Published by Triumph Books, Chicago.
Copyright © 2005 by Athlon Sports. All rights reserved.

Project Editors: Rob Doster, Mitch Light
Photo Editor: Tim Clark
Contributing Writers: George Schroeder, Carter Strickland

Content packaged by Mojo Media, Inc.
Editor: Joe Funk
Creative Director: Jason Hinman

No part of this publication may be reproduced, stored in a retrieval system, or transmitted, in any form by any means, electronic, mechanical, photocopying, or otherwise, without prior written permission of the publisher, Triumph Books, 601 S. LaSalle St., Suite 500, Chicago, Illinois 60605.

This book is available in quantity at special discounts for your group or organization.
For further information, contact:

Triumph Books
601 S. LaSalle St.
Suite 500
Chicago, Illinois 60605
Phone: (312) 939-3330
Fax: (312) 663-3557

Printed in the United States of America

Contents

Introduction 6
Big 12 Championship 10
Preseason
    Athlon's 2004 Oklahoma Preview 18
Regular Season 22
Features
    Adrian Peterson 36
    Jason White 54
    Bob Stoops 72
Postseason
    Orange Bowl 84
Traditions
    Oklahoma Football Tradition 90
    Sooner Spirit 96
Statistics 106
Roster 109

> After spending three months building an aura of invincibility, the 2003 Sooners had seen that aura evaporate — which makes what the 2004 Sooners accomplished that much more satisfying.

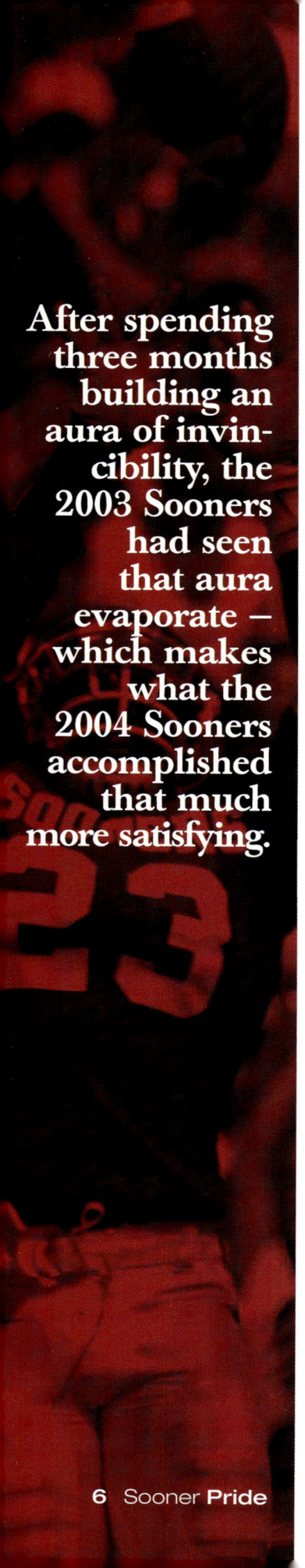

Introduction

Since the second half of the 20th Century began, no college football program — not Notre Dame, not Alabama, not Miami, not USC — can claim as much gridiron success as the Oklahoma Sooners. And with Bob Stoops at the helm and players like Adrian Peterson still eager to wear the Crimson and Cream, the Sooners show no signs of slowing anytime soon.

Given where the 2004 Sooners started, this season takes its place among the sweetest in OU's storied history.

With a late-season collapse, the 2003 Sooners had missed an opportunity to place their name among the greatest teams of all time. With that disappointment providing motivation, this year's team maintained its focus from beginning to end. An offseason of hard work, coupled with a renewed hunger (not to mention the arrival on campus of a certain freshman phenom), gave OU the necessary ingredients for another title run.

As odd as it sounds, the 2004 Sooners took on the persona of an underdog fighting for weekly respect. Expectations were high for this year's club, to be sure, but not as high as they had been in 2003, when the Sooners were a consensus preseason No. 1.

An air of doubt hung over this team. After all, hadn't we just seen Kansas State's Darren Sproles running wild vs. the Sooner defense in the 2003 Big 12 Championship Game? Hadn't Heisman Trophy winner Jason White looked like a rather ordinary quarterback in the humbling Sugar Bowl loss to LSU?

White in particular had more than his share of doubters, who wondered publicly whether the fair-haired QB had really deserved his Heisman Trophy. The defense, which was finally made to look vulnerable vs. K-State and LSU, had to be retooled after the loss of some key players. After spending three months building an aura of invincibility, the 2003 Sooners had seen that aura evaporate.

All of which makes what the 2004 Sooners accomplished that much more satisfying.

As 2004 unfolded, 2003's blowout wins were replaced by gut-checks. Facing teams that were motivated to avenge humiliating defeats, the Sooners took everyone's best shot. Whether it was a Texas team with a newfound toughness, or an Oklahoma State team with a history of derailing the Sooner Express, or a Texas A&M team pouring everything it had into erasing the memory of 77–0 — nothing came easy for this year's Sooners. They earned everything they got. And they earned the right to be called champions.

We're happy to celebrate their special season with them and with you. We don't expect it to be their last.

— The Editors

Sooner **Pride** 7

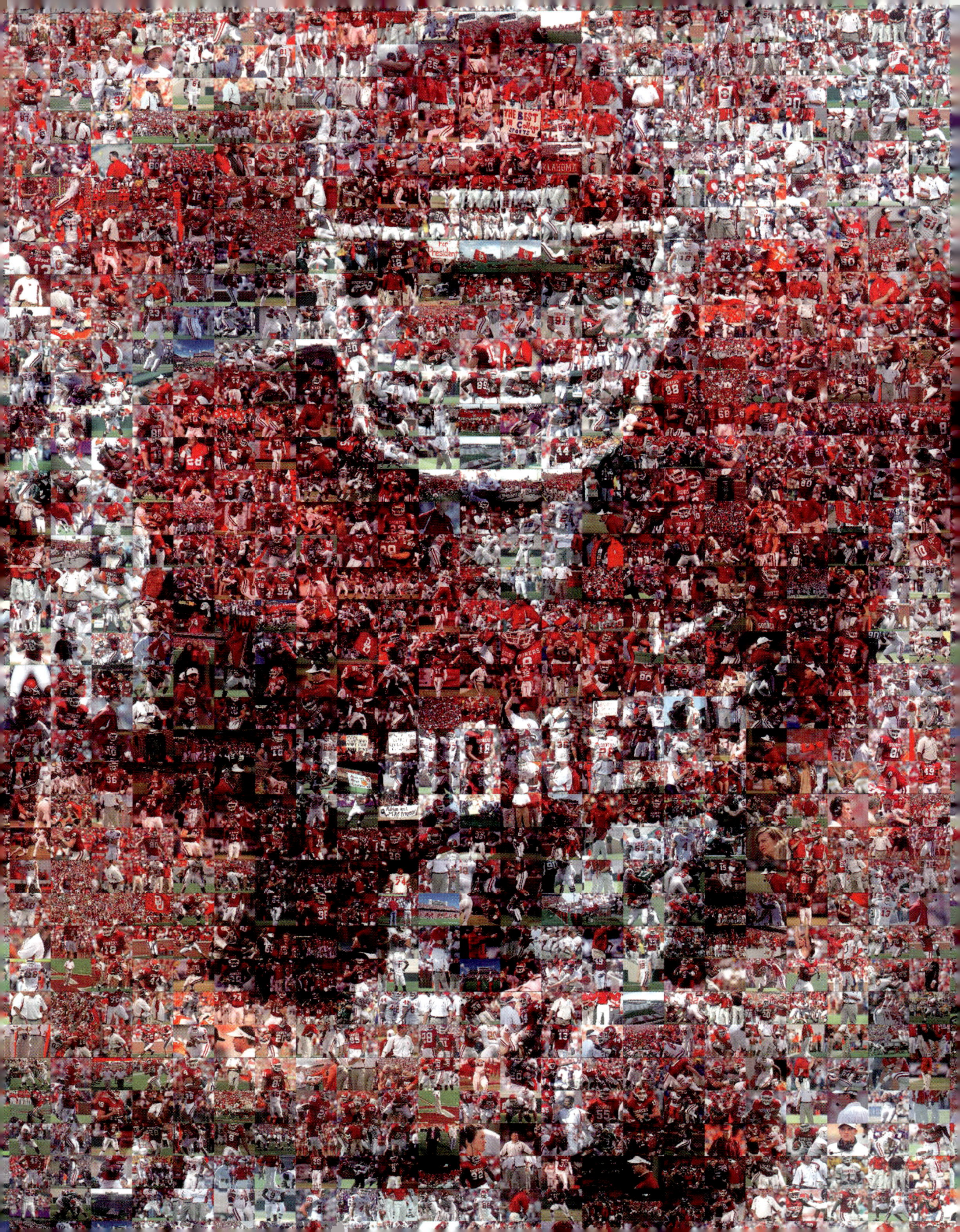

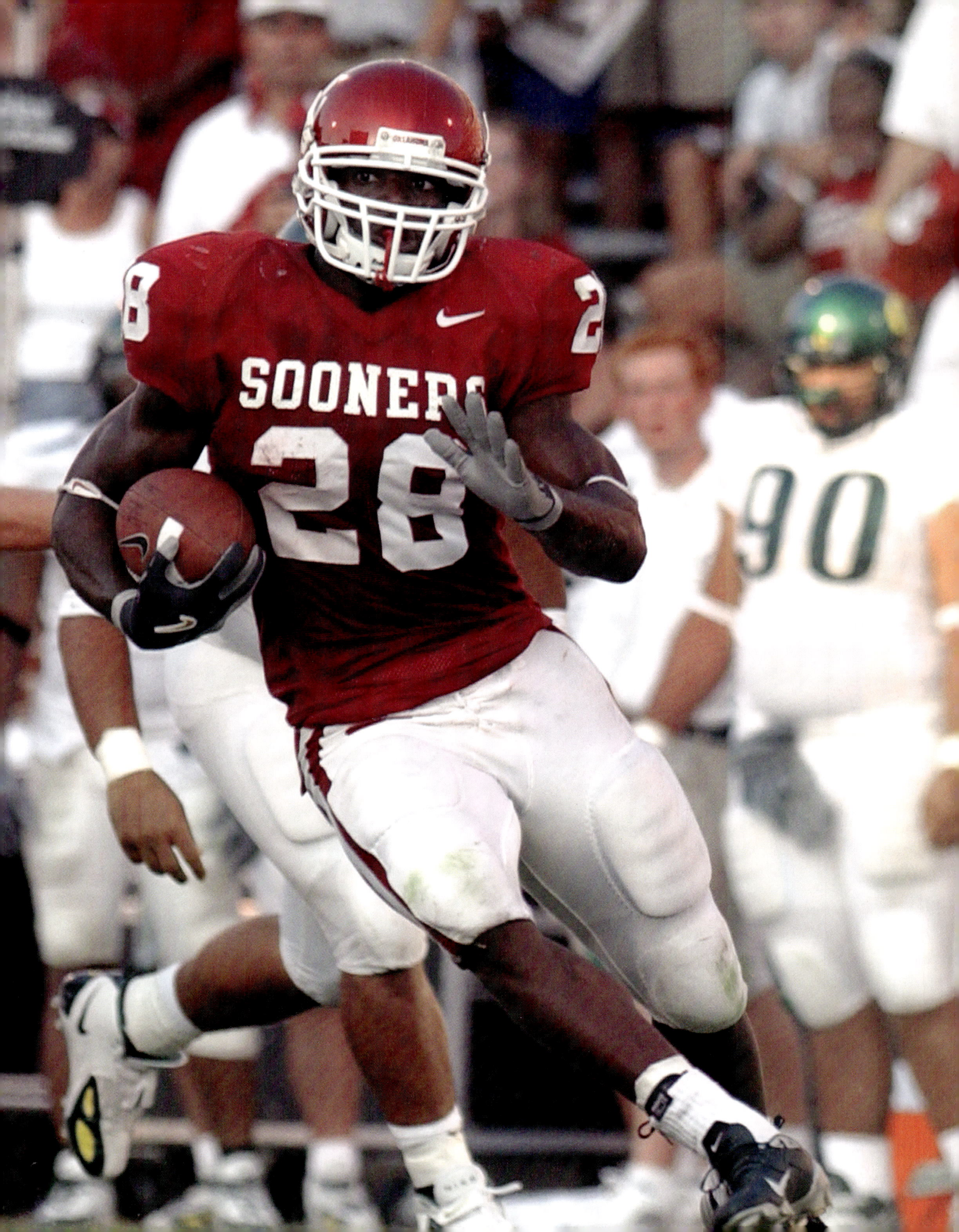
SOONERS
28
90

The 2004 Big 12 Championship

Photography by Larry Smith

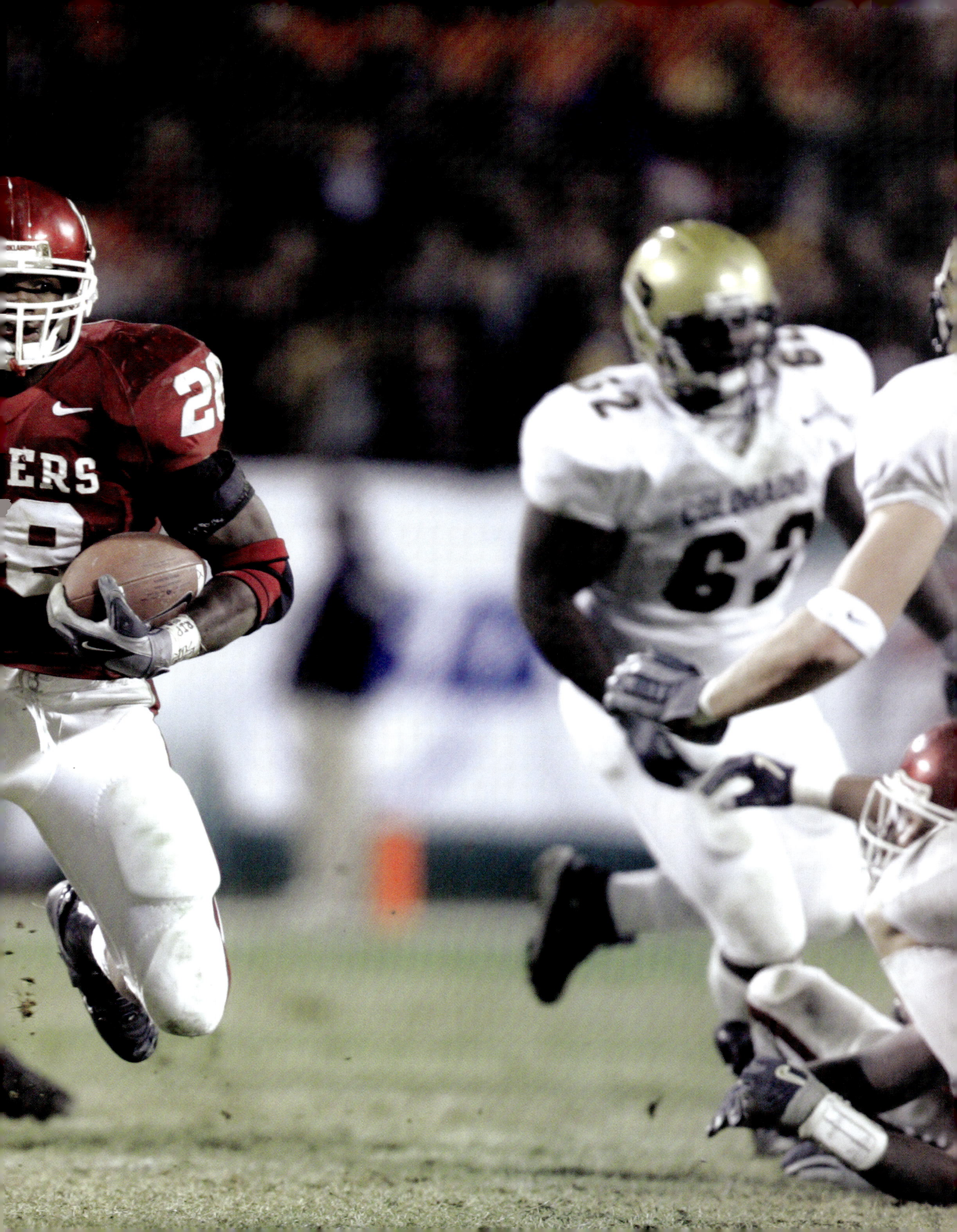

> "This is what it's all about. We're headed to the Orange Bowl."
> – DT Lawrence Dampeer

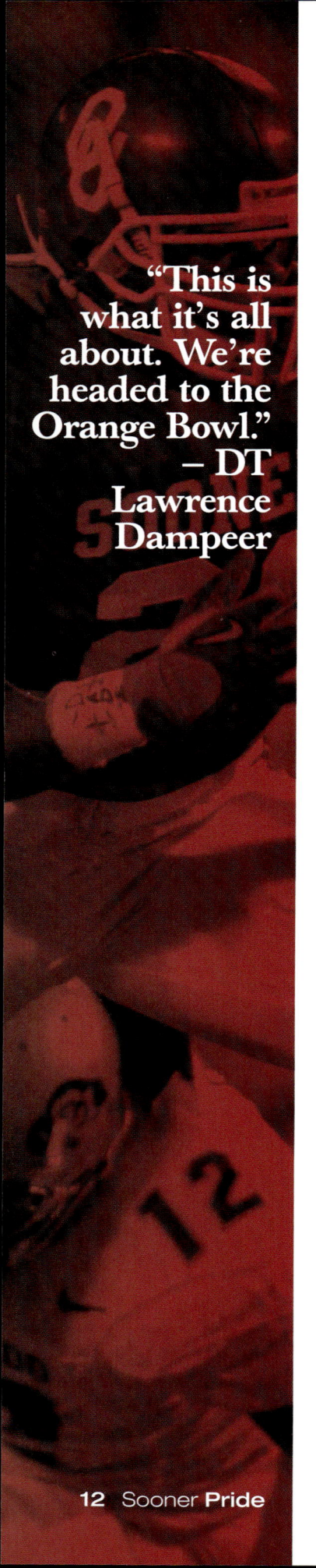

This Time, Sooners Finish the Job
Oklahoma 42, Colorado 3

Big 12 Championship Game, Dec. 4, 2004

KANSAS CITY, Mo. – As the oranges were tossed from the crowd and fell to the earth, Oklahoma's players walked around Arrowhead Stadium with their heads in the clouds.

This is what they had waited a year for — redemption, another trip to the national championship and a chance to prove they belonged.

"This is what it's all about," defensive tackle Lawrence "Moe" Dampeer screamed. "We're headed to the Orange Bowl."

This 42–3 win over Colorado in the Big 12 championship game was the sweetest victory of them all for Oklahoma.

"This is what we've been thinking about since the game ended last year," said fullback J.D. Runnels. "Every person on this team, everything we have done and talked about has been about coming back here. This is what we wanted ... we wanted another chance."

And there was no chance anyone was going to take it away from them. Not the number-crunchers in charge of the BCS computers, nor the human voters, coaches and media alike, nor Colorado. Least of all Colorado.

The Buffs could only play the role of hapless foil. Instead of the fight song, somebody should've cued circus music when the Biffs ran out of the tunnel.

"We didn't do anything," said CU coach Gary Barnett. "We didn't block well. We didn't flow well. We didn't run well. We didn't do any fundamentals the way they are supposed to be done, especially at a venue like this."

Even if Colorado had done some things well it wasn't likely Oklahoma was going to be stopped. This was a team that felt it was on a mission after losing the Big 12 championship and national title games last season.

"We made a statement today," said running back Adrian Peterson. "We went out and busted our butt for four quarters."

Actually it all started once the Sooners lost to Kansas State in last season's Big 12 title game. With that game fresh in their minds, the players started to talk about finishing strong. The finish motto was plastered everywhere. T-shirts were made. Finish lines were posted at the end of wind sprints. All season all the talk had been about finishing. And that meant finishing off CU.

The convincing fashion in which OU did finish the season may have quelled some of the doubters who ranked Auburn ahead of the Sooners in the polls. Not that where they were ranked or how highly they were thought of mattered all that much to some players.

"We are not making any statements when we go out and win a championship except to

---

Adrian Peterson: "We made a statement today. We went out and busted our butt for four quarters."

Photography by Larry Smith

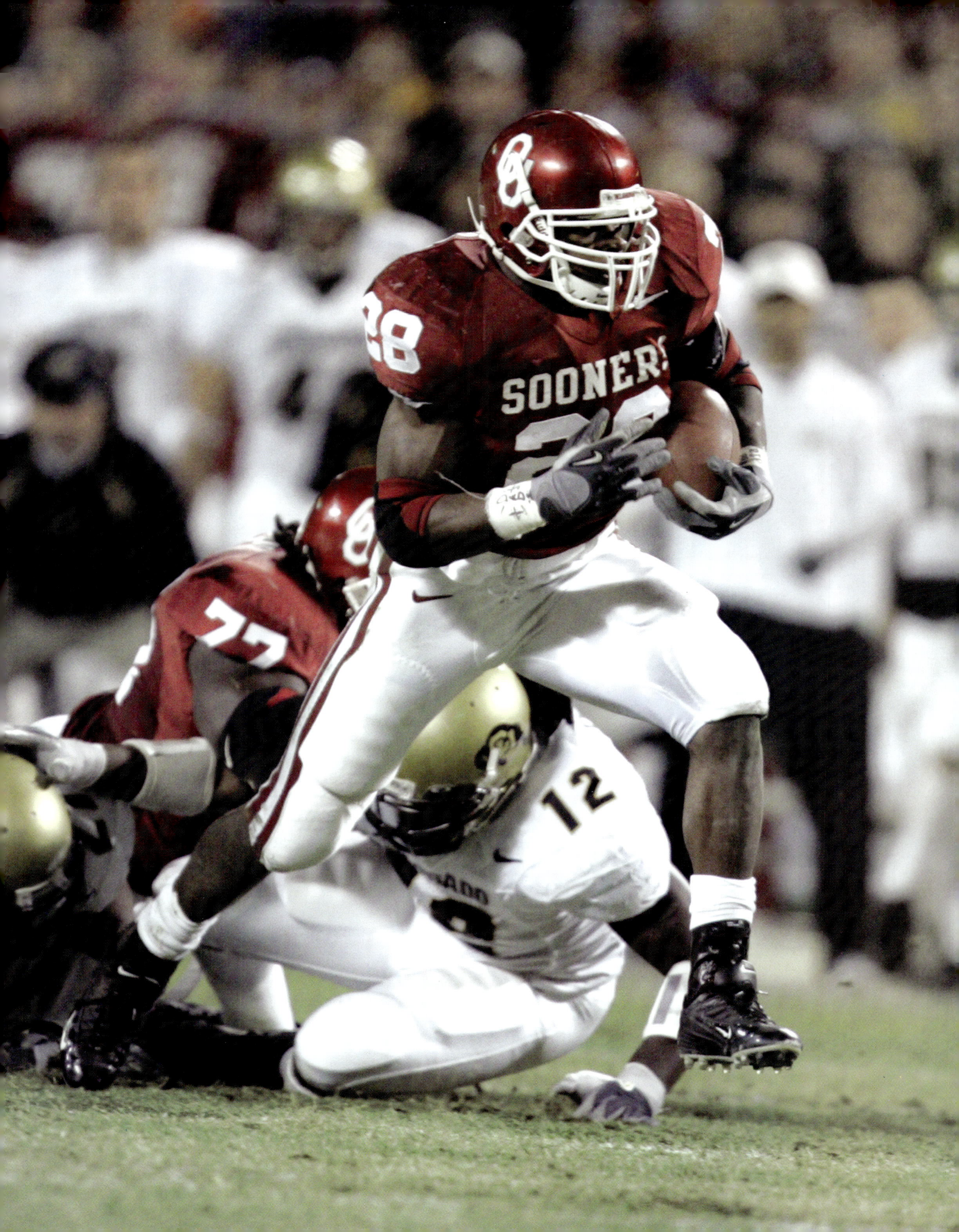

SOONERS
28
77
12

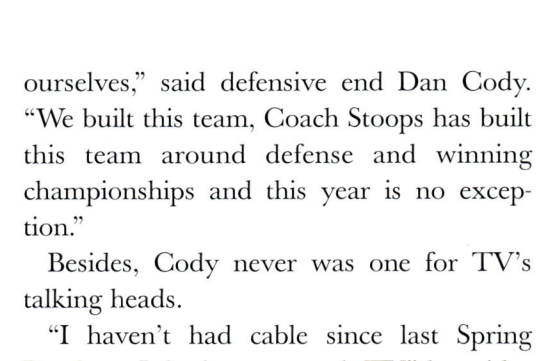

ourselves," said defensive end Dan Cody. "We built this team, Coach Stoops has built this team around defense and winning championships and this year is no exception."

Besides, Cody never was one for TV's talking heads.

"I haven't had cable since last Spring Break, so I don't even watch TV," he said.

Stoops, the highest-paid coach in college football, can certainly afford cable and was in tune with what was going on around the country. The coach lobbied – not so subtly – for his team during the weeks preceding the Big 12 title game. But Oklahoma made its most convincing argument with actions, not words.

"For some reason people, maybe they don't like Oklahoma or whatever," said defensive tackle Lynn McGruder. "Maybe they don't want to see us where we are. But we're back."

This year's OU squad finished what it started.

Photography by Larry Smith

14 Sooner Pride

Sooner **Pride** 15

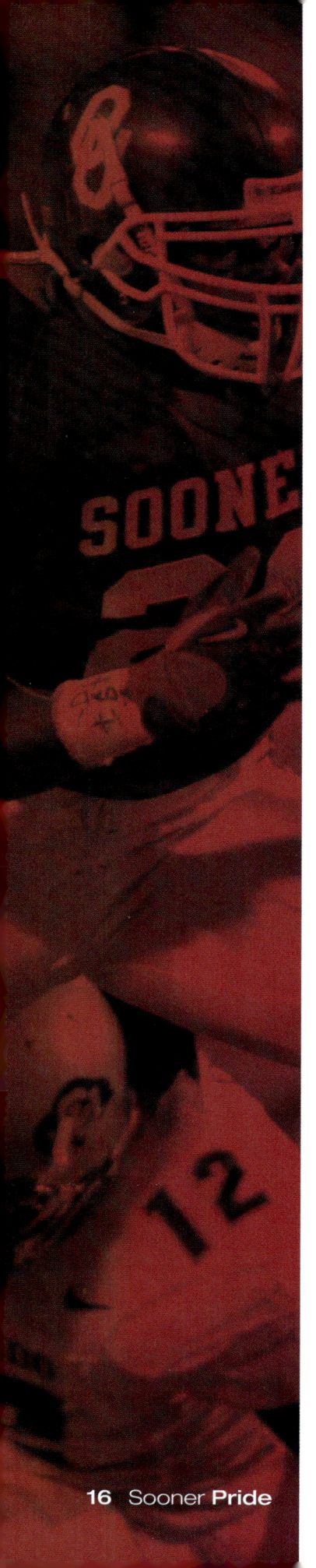

Oklahoma scored on four of its first five drives to take a 28–0 lead. Those scores came off drives of 80, 63, 53 and 40 yards. The play of quarterback Jason White (22-of-29 for 254 yards, two interceptions and three touchdowns) put the senior right back at the center of the Heisman race.

"(The voters) are going to look at this game and see what he did, especially early," Oklahoma offensive coordinator Chuck Long said. "He finished with a high percentage and a good efficiency. And with how many points we scored, they will look at that very seriously."

As for White, like he has done all season, he deflected talk of the Heisman.

"I'm just trying to win," he said. "Those individual awards are great. Words can't speak to all the fun it is to be there. (But) right now I'm enjoying the victory. That's one of the main reasons I came back."

White also apparently wasn't going back to campus without one thing.

"I'm not coming back without that trophy," White told Long in the week that preceded the Big 12 Championship game.

White was committed, but he wasn't perfect. The senior did throw two inconsequential interceptions. The first one came on an ill-advised throw into the end zone. Willie Roberts, a 6'7" tight end, went out for a fade route. White's ball faded about two feet before it got to Roberts. Terrence Wheatley, all 5'10" of him, picked the pass.

It was tough to find fault with White on the second pick. On a field with the traction of an oil slick, wide receiver Mark Bradley slipped on his route, and the ball went into the hands of Colorado's Lorenzo Sims. The pick set up Colorado's only points of the game. It also marked the one and only time CU got into Oklahoma territory.

As for Oklahoma, it was in CU territory all day, thanks largely in part to a player whose nickname is A.D., or All Day – Adrian Peterson. The freshman finished with 172 yards, the last 32 of which came on a spinning, twisting touchdown dash on which he broke six tackles.

Another thing Peterson broke was the NCAA freshman record for 100-yard rushing games. He had 11 of them in the 12-game season. The only game in which Peterson didn't equal or surpass 100 yards came when he sat out half the game against Nebraska with a shoulder injury. He also moved into third place on OU's single-season rushing chart with 1,843 yards. And with three touchdowns, Peterson set a record for touchdowns scored (15) by a freshman at OU.

After the first four carries it was apparent it would be Peterson's night. The 6-2, 215-pound Palestine, Texas, product had 50 yards on the first four carries.

"We came out and we hit them fast," said offensive lineman Chris Bush. "We knew that if we came out and attacked that line we could run on them."

The Sooners also knew that in Peterson, they had just the back to do it.

"I have never seen a guy that big, that strong, that fast," said CU's Terrence Wheatley.

Meanwhile, the first time CU got a first down not by penalty was in the third quarter. Quarterback Joel Klatt threw for a total of 52 yards, and running back Bobby Purify had just seven yards.

"There is no question we are embarrassed by our performance," Barnett said. "We were inept at best. We played a very, very good football team and we were just not prepared to play that team today."

Oklahoma, on the other hand, was ready. Both offensively and defensively.

"To be in a championship game and to play this way defensively was so impressive," Stoops said. "The guys were just sound. There were no busts, they tackled well and the defensive line got penetration."

When Klatt did try and throw, Dampeer dropped back and batted the ball down.

"He looked like a DB out there," Stoops said of the 300-plus-pound freshman.

Dampeer wasn't the only player who

changed roles. Even though they didn't need it, the Sooners decided to roll out a trick. Up 28–0 and faced with a 30-yard field goal, holder Mark Bradley took the snap, bounced through Colorado and picked up the first down. But it was all for naught as White threw an interception in the end zone the next play. It was the first pick White had thrown in 199 pass attempts.

As for Bradley, who also plays wide receiver and returns kicks, it was thought the Sooners would use him as a threat on the field goal team earlier in the season. But he never did anything but hold – until the Big 12 title game. Oklahoma might have showed the play to plant a seed of uneasiness in the minds of its Orange Bowl opponents. But in doing so, the Sooners let an opportunity get away for kicker Garrett Hartley.

Hartley, a true freshman, took over the kicking duties from Trey DiCarlo in the Baylor game. Against the Bears, he only got point after attempts. When the Sooners passed on the field goal attempt against Colorado, they set up a scenario where Hartley's first kick could come on the biggest stage in college football – the BCS title game.

Of course, in the hoopla that ensued after the win over Colorado, no Sooner was worried about the game plan for the Orange Bowl. Instead, they were content to soak up the hysteria.

"We all know how well Oklahoma does in the Orange Bowl, and we feel like we are capable of doing well there too," said return man Antonio Perkins.

Stoops, always confident, had that feeling as well.

"This team isn't missing any parts," he said. "I believe we are solid all the way through. Offensively, we have the balance, ability to make the plays, running or throwing and make a lot of big plays that way.

"Our defense has been very good through 12 games," Stoops said. "There are a couple of games where we gave up a few passes. The rest of the teams we have played awfully well."

And only one hurdle remained before the job at hand was truly finished. ■

stats

Score by Quarters	1	2	3	4	Score	
Colorado	0	0	3	0	3	Record: (7-5,4-4)
Oklahoma	14	14	7	7	42	Record: (12-0,8-0)

Scoring Summary:
1st 10:21 OU - Peoples, Will 5 yd pass from White, Jason (Hartley, Garret kick), 11-80 4:39, CU 0 - OU 7
05:29 OU - Clayton, Mark 22 yd pass from White, Jason (Hartley, Garret kick), 6-63 2:28, CU 0 - OU 14
2nd 14:53 OU - Clayton, Mark 22 yd pass from White, Jason (Hartley, Garret kick), 8-53 3:53, CU 0 - OU 21
06:06 OU - Peterson, Adrian 1 yd run (Hartley, Garret kick), 8-40 4:15, CU 0 - OU 28
3rd 09:53 OU - Peterson, Adrian 3 yd run (Hartley, Garret kick), 8-26 4:00, CU 0 - OU 35
02:01 CU - Crosby, Mason 34 yd field goal, 5-16 2:09, CU 3 - OU 35
4th 12:53 OU - Peterson, Adrian 32 yd run (Hartley, Garret kick), 7-66 4:02, CU 3 - OU 42

	CU	OU
FIRST DOWNS	3	26
RUSHES-YARDS (NET)	16—4	46-236
PASSING YDS (NET)	50	262
Passes Att-Comp-Int	28-9-1	32-24-2
TOTAL OFFENSE PLAYS-YARDS	44-46	78-498
Fumble Returns-Yards	0-0	0-0
Punt Returns-Yards	2-2	4-16
Kickoff Returns-Yards	6-105	1-33
Interception Returns-Yards	2-34	1-0
Punts (Number-Avg)	9-43.6	4-38.8
Fumbles-Lost	0-0	1-1
Penalties-Yards	6-37	9-90
Possession Time	20:28	39:32
Third-Down Conversions	0 of 12	11 of 16
Fourth-Down Conversions	0 of 1	1 of 1
Red-Zone Scores-Chances	1-1	3-4
Sacks By: Number-Yards	0-0	3-14

RUSHING: Colorado-Purify, Bobby 12-7; Ellis, Byron 1-3; Klatt, Joel 3-minus 14. Oklahoma-Peterson, Adrian 28-172; Hickson, Donta 8-33; Jones, Kejuan 7-16; Clayton, Mark 2-9; Bradley, Mark 1-6.

PASSING: Colorado-Klatt, Joel 8-26-1-52; Cox, James 0-1-0-0; Torp, John 1-1-0-minus 2. Oklahoma-White, Jason 22-29-2-254; Grady, Tommy 2-3-0-8.

RECEIVING: Colorado-Mackey, Blake 2-14; Judge, Evan 1-10; Littlehales,Tyl 1-8; Purify, Bobby 1-7; Sprague, Dusty 1-6; Duren, Mike 1-4; Monteilh, Ron 1-3; Brooks,Dominiqu 1-minus 2. Oklahoma-Clayton, Mark 8-106; Wilson, Travis 5-72; Bradley, Mark 4-46; Jones, Kejuan 3-12; Runnels, J.D. 1-13; Jones, Brandon 1-6; Peoples, Will 1-5; Finley, Joe Jon 1-2.

INTERCEPTIONS: Colorado-Sims, Lorenzo 1-34; Wheatley,Terren 1-0. Oklahoma-Perkins, Antoni 1-0.

FUMBLES: Colorado-None. Oklahoma-Clayton, Mark 1-1.

Athlon Sports Big Twelve Football Preview 2004

OKLAHOMA SOONERS

National Forecast: 2 **Big 12 South Prediction: 1st**

To listen last winter to Oklahoma fans — and sometimes players — you'd have thought the Sooners' 2003 season was a disaster. There wasn't any dwelling on a 12–0 start. The losing streak — at two games, it matches the longest in the Bob Stoops era — dominated conversation. Just ask quarterback Jason White, who won the Heisman Trophy but was denied a championship.

"It definitely put a damper on the whole season," White says.

And fueled the Sooners' resolve for 2004. "I think the whole team's more hungry," he says.

Here's the good news for Oklahoma fans: The Sooners return the nucleus of the unit that pursued history through 12 games last season. The Sooners return nine offensive starters from a unit that set the school record for scoring, averaging 42.9 points per game. And with the arrival of a freshman phenom at tailback, the running game — a weakness in 2003 — should be strengthened.

OU must replace three national award winners from its defense. But the Sooners believe they've reached the point of reloading, not rebuilding.

It all points to another run at the national championship. "We've got a lot of guys back," Stoops says. "I would think we've got about as good a shot as anybody."

Quarterbacks

White was a senior last season, but a few days after winning the Heisman, he announced he had applied for a sixth year of eligibility from the NCAA. Because he missed most of 2001 and 2002 with knee injuries, he was eligible. He becomes the first Heisman winner with a shot to repeat since BYU's Ty Detmer in 1991.

White, who had 40 touchdowns and 10 interceptions — 40 and six in the 12–0 regular season — should be more mobile than last season, when he struggled at times with those creaky knees.

And while coaches don't expect him to match the otherworldly statistics, they believe he might just be a better, savvier quarterback than he was in 2003.

Coaches are considering redshirting junior backup Paul Johnson this season, giving him two seasons as a potential starter beginning in 2005. That might also give some playing time to redshirt freshman Tommy Grady. True freshman Rhett Bomar, possibly the nation's top prep quarterback, is expected to redshirt.

Running Backs

Adrian Peterson was considered the nation's top high school player by most recruiting services last season. If he's as good as the hype — and coaches who typically don't overhype say he is — the 6'2", 210-pound combination of power and speed could be the immediate key that unlocks the running game.

That said, junior Kejuan Jones was impressive in the spring. After rushing for 925 yards in 2003 while splitting time with now-departed Renaldo Works, Jones added muscle weight and decreased his 40 time last winter. And yes, Jones knows the challenge that's coming from Peterson. "I'm not just gonna give up the position just like that," he says.

Donta Hickson, Tashard Choice and true freshman D.J. Wolfe will also get looks in the preseason. But the competition likely will come down to Jones and Peterson.

Receivers

Statistically, OU returns its top five receivers. How to juggle the catches? "We've got six or seven guys that can really play," receivers coach Darrell Wyatt says.

Mark Clayton's breakout year overshadowed a deep, talented group. In addition to Clayton, Brandon Jones (46 catches, 709 yards, eight TDs), Jejuan Rankins (33 catches, six TDs), Will Peoples (24 catches, three TDs) and Travis Wilson (25 catches, four TDs) all return.

One positive development last spring was the emergence of OU's tight ends.

Post-Spring Analysis

Keys to a National Championship

The loss in the Sugar Bowl to LSU denied the Sooners the national championship — or a piece of it, anyway. But OU appears primed for another run at a title. Nine offensive starters return, including Heisman winner Jason White and his entire stable of wide receivers. The biggest offensive upgrade could be at tailback, where true freshman Adrian Peterson will get every opportunity to win a job and make an immediate impact. Defensively, OU lost three All-Americans. But it appears the Sooners have reached the point where they can reload, not rebuild. The defense might not be quite as good as last year's, or at least not as star-studded. But a slight drop-off would still be a tough challenge for opposing offenses. "We have the capability of being better than we were last year," White says.

2004 Schedule

S. 4	Bowling Green	W
S. 11	Houston	W
S. 18	Oregon	W
O. 2	Texas Tech	W
O. 9	**#Texas**	*
O. 16	at Kansas State	W
O. 23	Kansas	W
O. 30	at Oklahoma State	W
N. 6	at Texas A&M	W
N. 13	Nebraska	W
N. 20	at Baylor	W
#Dallas, TX		

*Games in bold represent games crucial to the season.
W or L indicates a projected win or loss

Mark Clayton: 83 catches, 1,425 yards, 15 touchdowns in '03

18 Sooner **Pride**

Jason White

Athlon Sports Big Twelve Football Preview 2004

Antonio Perkins

James "Bubba" Moses served notice he's ready to combine blocking ability with receiving skills. Joe Jon Finley and Willie Roberts, though less complete, both showed promise as well.

Offensive Linemen

All five starters return from a unit that provided stout protection for White for most of the year, but faltered late. Two starters — center Vince Carter and tackle Wes Sims — will begin their fourth seasons as starters, and Jammal Brown, the other tackle, is in his third season as a starter. At guard, juniors Davin Joseph and Kelvin Chaisson are solid veterans.

NUMBERS GAME

4 OU has beaten archrival Texas four years in a row, matching the longest winning streak by either team since the Sooners won five straight in 1971-75.

Brown and Carter, consensus All-Big 12 picks in 2003, should vie for All-America honors. Brown led the unit with 127 knockdown blocks.

The Sooners are thin; if injuries strike, unproven youngsters will have to step in.

Defensive Linemen

Tommie Harris left a big gap when he jumped early to the NFL. Or did he?

There were whispers last season that Dusty Dvoracek (now a senior) was the Sooners' best tackle. Dvoracek, who had seven sacks and 16 tackles for loss, should fill Harris' void. "At times, he's been unblockable," co-defensive coordinator Brent Venables says. "Dusty seems to be a guy on a mission."

Not to be left out are OU's defensive ends. Dan Cody and Jonathan Jackson might be as good a pass-rushing twosome as there is.

Back on the interior, Lynn McGruder was also a regular in the Sooners' four-man defensive rotation. After those mainstays, several newcomers will get a chance to play; junior college transfer Remi Ayodele might be counted on most.

Linebackers

At one point, Venables expected to have to replace all three linebackers this season. Instead, he needed to find just one.

When standout middle linebacker Lance Mitchell blew out a knee in the third game last season, Gayron Allen was thrust into a more prominent role. Now, Mitchell is back, bringing "stability," according to Venables. And the experience gained last season by Allen should allow him to comfortably slip into the weakside linebacker position formerly occupied by Butkus winner Teddy Lehman.

Venables spent much of the spring trying to identify a strong-side linebacker and believes he found one in junior Clint Ingram. In recent years, OU hasn't often used the position, preferring instead to go with extra defensive backs. But Ingram and his backups might give OU a more athletic presence and the ability to remain on the field in passing situations.

Defensive Backs

Though OU returns three starters, the loss of cornerback Derrick Strait might hurt the defense most. "Derrick was so valuable in so many ways with his playmaking ability and consistency," Venables says.

Several players will compete for Strait's spot as the short-side corner. Eric Bassey, a backup in 2003, and Chijioke Onyenegecha, a talented junior college transfer, will get the longest looks.

At safety, Donte Nicholson is solid. And Brodney Pool appears poised for a breakout season; Sooner insiders compare him to former OU standout Roy Williams.

Specialists

Two years ago, Trey DiCarlo stepped out of a car and won an open tryout for the Sooners' placekicking duties. A finalist for the Lou Groza award last season, DiCarlo is firmly entrenched as a reliable weapon.

In the return game, Perkins returns with his eyes on the NCAA's career punt-return touchdown record. He took back three for TDs in a win last season against UCLA. Though many opponents choose to kick away from Perkins to take away the home run threat, the strategy typically results in good field position for the Sooners anyway.

Blake Ferguson returns for his third season as punter.

RISING STAR

At City College of San Francisco, **Chijioke Onyenegecha** was considered one of the top junior college cornerbacks. At 6'2", 205 pounds, he combines outstanding size with sprinters' speed. Onyenegecha spent spring practice on the second team. But coaches expect him to have a significant impact this fall.

Outside the Huddle

Schedule upgrade The biggest off-season moves were made by OU athletic director Joe Castiglione, who revised a non-conference schedule of Bowling Green, Arkansas State and Florida A&M, replacing the latter two teams with Oregon and Houston.

Pelini arrives Mike Stoops' departure and the arrival of Bo Pelini could make for one of the more interesting subplots. Pelini, who was Nebraska's defensive coordinator (and interim head coach for the Alamo Bowl win), is co-defensive coordinator at OU. Brent Venables also holds that title — and ultimate control of defensive decisions. The relationship appears to be working, but bears watching.

Defensive dominance In the last four years OU has ranked in the top 25 of five key defensive categories: total defense, scoring defense, rushing defense, passing defense and pass efficiency defense.

Secret weapon Senior walk-on Mark Bradley — son of former OU quarterback Danny Bradley — made a mark as a receiver last season. Though the receiving rotation is crowded, Bradley's big-play ability didn't go unnoticed. Bradley, a former high school quarterback who threw a touchdown pass on a reverse last year, will hold on extra points and field goals, thereby giving the Sooners another option on fakes.

The first time, Oregon was flagged for illegal substitution. The second time, OU was called for too many players on the field.

"I couldn't help but laugh myself," Stoops said.

There was nothing for the Sooners to laugh about in the third quarter as Oregon came out and made the game a little tighter with a nine-play, 80-yard drive that ended in a 30-yard touchdown pass to Dante Rosario. That made it 17–7 with plenty of time for the Ducks' potent offense to add to its total.

"The third and fourth quarter, particularly the third, we eased up a little bit," said OU linebacker Lance Mitchell. "That's where they got us."

The Sooners were also lacking depth on the defensive line. Senior Dusty Dvoracek was kicked off the team the Friday night before the game for a series of transgressions that involved alcohol and violence. The players said they were stunned by the move, but chose to move on.

After the quick Duck drive, the OU defense did move on with some help from Oregon. The Ducks' own mistakes stopped any chance Oregon had of an upset.

"For about a half or three quarters I was proud of this team," Bellotti said. "We battled. I don't think we battled in the fourth quarter. I was disappointed with our performance there."

"We underachieved," added Oregon quarterback Kellen Clemens, who was 24-of-35 for 179 yards. "We're not playing to our potential. Offensively we need to finish when we have the opportunities to score. The penalties and the sacks, they hurt us."

OU held Oregon's normally potent offense to 321 yards on 71 plays for an average of 4.5 yards per play. OU countered with a 6.2-yard average.

"They had phenomenal team speed," Clemens said. "They are a very, very good defense. They read the screen game very well today."

With OU's defense keeping Oregon in check, the offense turned to Peterson in the late stages of the game. The freshman wore down the Oregon defense and ran down the game clock as he took handoff after handoff on two scoring drives. His touchdowns of 40 and 18 yards extended the lead to 31–7.

"That's what we focused on this offseason, establishing the run game," said White. "There's still room for improvement." ■

stats

Score by Quarters	1	2	3	4	Score	
University of Oregon	0	0	7	0	7	Record: (0-2)
Oklahoma Sooners	0	10	14	7	31	Record: (3-0)

Scoring Summary:

2nd 14:56 OU - DiCarlo, Trey 35 yd field goal, 12-49 5:10, ORE 0 - OU 3
 06:03 OU - Moses, James 4 yd pass from White, Jason (DiCarlo, Trey kick), 10-74 3:24, ORE 0 - OU 10
3rd 07:47 OU - Hickson, Donta 25 yd run (DiCarlo, Trey kick), 9-90 4:33, ORE 0 - OU 17
 04:15 ORE - Rosario, Dante 30 yd pass from Clemens, Kellen (Siegel, Jared kick), 9-80 3:32, ORE 7 - OU 17
 01:15 OU - Peterson, Adrian 40 yd run (DiCarlo, Trey kick), 7-79 2:53, ORE 7 - OU 24
4th 03:36 OU - Peterson, Adrian 18 yd run (DiCarlo, Trey kick), 7-89 2:51, ORE 7 - OU 31

	ORE	OU
FIRST DOWNS	20	27
RUSHES-YARDS (NET)	34-140	46-214
PASSING YDS (NET)	181	213
Passes Att-Comp-Int	37-25-0	23-17-0
TOTAL OFFENSE PLAYS-YARDS	71-321	69-427
Fumble Returns-Yards	1-8	0-0
Punt Returns-Yards	2-7	2-22
Kickoff Returns-Yards	3-60	2-45
Interception Returns-Yards	0-0	0-0
Punts (Number-Avg)	6-40.8	4-43.8
Fumbles-Lost	1-1	2-1
Penalties-Yards	11-100	6-45
Possession Time	28:37	31:23
Third-Down Conversions	4 of 14	9 of 14
Fourth-Down Conversions	2 of 3	0 of 0
Red-Zone Scores-Chances	0-2	3-4
Sacks By: Number-Yards	2-14	2-14

RUSHING: University of Oregon-Whitehead, T. 13-66; Washington, Ken 9-30; Allen, Keith 1-25; Colvin, Cameron 1-8; Clemens, Kellen 8-7; Dixon, Dennis 1-4; Siegel, Jared 1-0. Oklahoma Sooners-Peterson, Adrian 24-183; Jones, Kejuan 11-41; Hickson, Donta 2-19; Wolfe, D.J. 3-3; TEAM 1-minus 1; White, Jason 5-minus 31.

PASSING: University of Oregon-Clemens, Kellen 24-35-0-179; Dixon, Dennis 1-2-0-2. Oklahoma Sooners-White, Jason 17-23-0-213.

RECEIVING: University of Oregon-Rosario, Dante 7-64; Williams, D. 6-36; Whitehead, T. 4-19; Maxwell, Marcus 3-27; Day, Tim 2-22; Washington, Ken 2-12; Strong, Garren 1-1. Oklahoma Sooners-Clayton, Mark 6-91; Jones, Brandon 3-46; Hickson, Donta 2-minus 3; Jones, Kejuan 1-23; Wilson, Travis 1-20; Bradley, Mark 1-17; Runnels, J.D. 1-10; Peoples, Will 1-5; Moses, James 1-4.

INTERCEPTIONS: University of Oregon-None. Oklahoma Sooners-None.

FUMBLES: University of Oregon-Clemens, Kellen 1-1. Oklahoma Sooners-Clayton, Mark 1-0; White, Jason 1-1.

"It's his strength, it's his speed, it's his vision, it's toughness when he takes somebody on. He's got it all."
– Bob Stoops

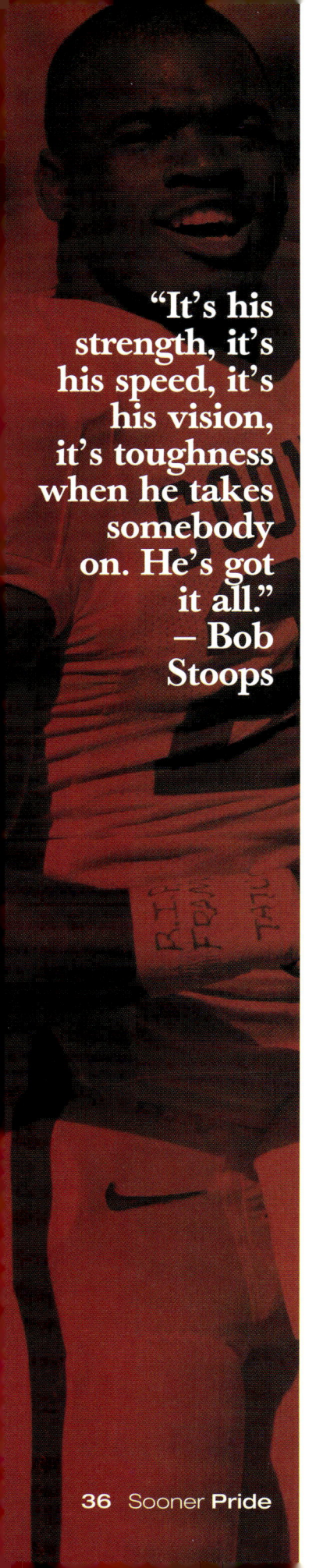

Unflappable Peterson Sets New Freshman Standard

NORMAN, Okla. – Adrian Peterson didn't live up to the hype.

He exceeded it.

Considered the nation's top recruit of the 2004 class, Peterson arrived at Oklahoma with plenty of accolades. Expectations were high.

But no one – no one – expected what happened. Peterson's freshman season ranks among the best by any freshman, at OU or anywhere else. And through it all, through the 100-yard games and the ESPN SportsCenter highlights and the Heisman hype and the national championship and all of that, the freshman appeared completely unfazed.

Even when reporters surrounded him, shoving notebooks and cameras into his face. Even when autograph-seekers stalked him, hiding in bushes and popping out to demand a signature and a picture.

And especially when defenders pestered him, trying (often in vain) to tackle him.

"It's kind of crazy," Peterson said. "I just try to take everything in stride. I really don't let anything bother me much."

Well, no. Apparently not. And it's easy to see why, considering the youngster's background.

Consider, for a moment, that as a 7-year-old, Peterson watched as his 11-year-old brother, Brian, was killed by a drunk driver while riding his bike. Note that his father, Nelson Peterson, has been in federal prison since 1999 for laundering drug money. Adrian Peterson was a seventh-grader when his father went to prison.

"I think about my brother and I think about my dad," Adrian said. "I wish they were both still here, but things happen for a reason, I feel. I get sad about different things sometimes, but I try to use it to motivate me, to keep me going."

And somehow, maybe, Peterson's past fused with his talent, helping produce the maturity that allowed him to handle the attention and adulation that came along with sudden stardom.

"Most freshmen don't have the ability to handle everything he has," OU coach Bob Stoops said. "I think it's a process with him, with all the media attention and the fanfare and people that are after him. You've got to keep growing with it and understand it, and he has.

"He's got a great ability to not get caught up in it. He has that kind of mental strength to handle it."

There might have been another reason. OU running backs coach Cale Gundy suggested Peterson might have been sheltered a bit during the season by youthful naivete.

"He's still a kid. He's a 19-year-old kid who loves playing football," Gundy said. "He has come to an understanding of what he's been through this year, having the suc-

Virtually everything about Adrian Peterson's freshman season — from his second-place Heisman finish to his remarkable numbers to his uncommon poise — was unprecedented.

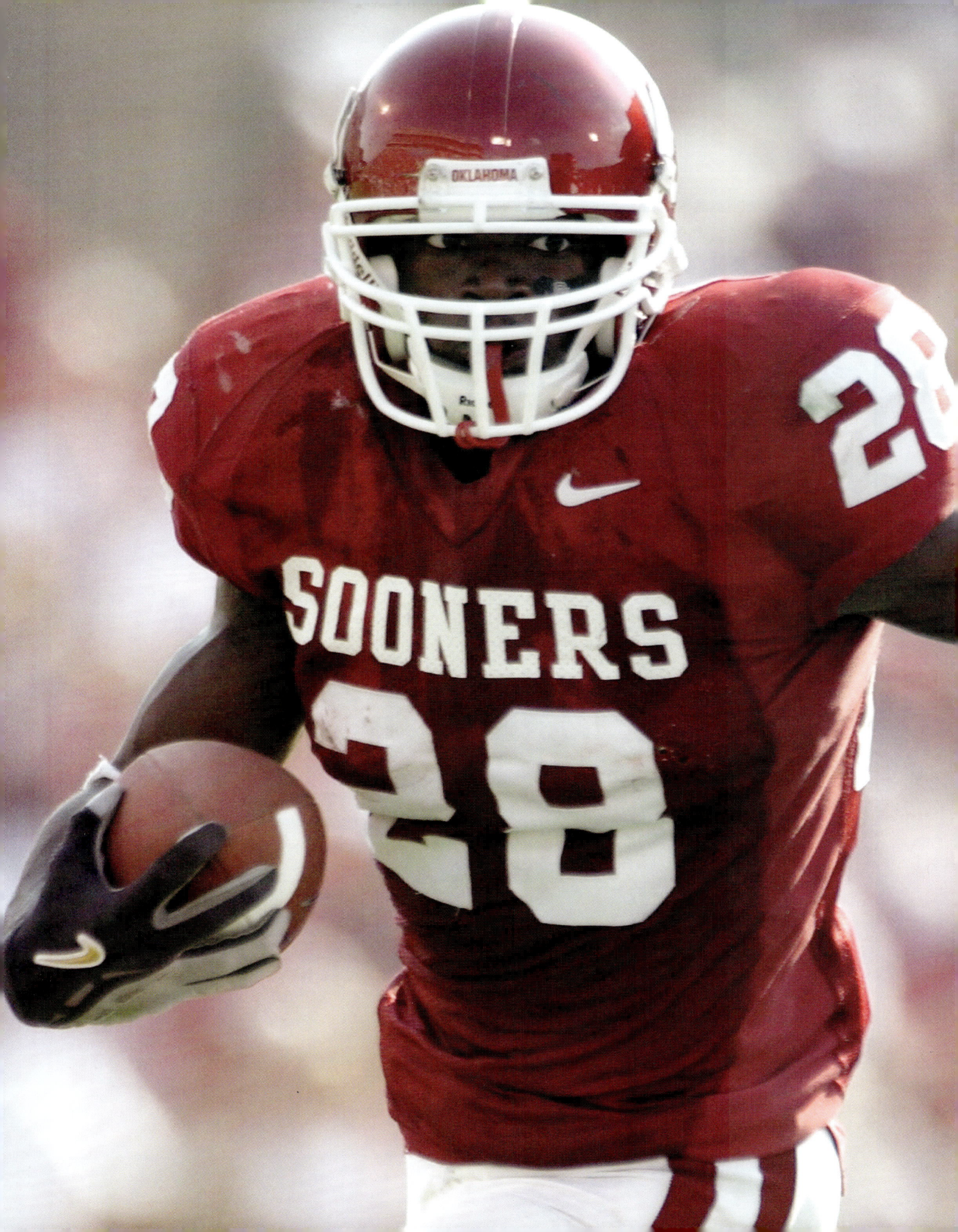
OKLAHOMA
SOONERS
28
28

cess and the awards and all of that. But I think just still being a kid has helped protect him from some of it."

The 6-foot-2, 210-pound combination of power and speed raced through his first season as a man among boys. En route to a Heisman runner-up finish — the highest finish by a freshman in the history of the coveted award — Peterson drew comparisons to all-time greats: Herschel Walker, Billy Sims, Eric Dickerson, and on and on.

In reality, he combined attributes of all of them, and more.

"It's his strength, it's his speed, it's his vision, it's toughness when he takes somebody on," Stoops said. "He's got it all."

Peterson rushed for at least 100 yards in each of his first nine games, establishing an NCAA freshman record. The streak ended when Peterson had 58 yards in limited action against Nebraska while nursing an injured shoulder. But in 12 games (with the Orange Bowl remaining), Peterson had rushed for 100 yards in 11 of them.

He had filled up highlight reels en route to 1,843 yards and 15 touchdowns.

"As I continued, I got better and better," Peterson said. "I learned a lot more about the game. The biggest thing for me was really just slowing down and letting things develop."

And Peterson's performances in big games told the story. Against the three ranked opponents OU faced during the regular season — all on the road — Peterson averaged 191.3 yards.

"He's one of those clutch guys, one off those guys that rises to the occasion," offensive coordinator Chuck Long said.

"I think maybe he gets a little more challenged," Gundy said. "In certain situations, I think he kicks it up a gear. And I think maybe, deep down inside him, he knows to win these big games, 'I've definitely got to do my part.' And he puts a little extra in it."

He rushed for 225 against Texas, 249 against Oklahoma State and 101 against Texas A&M. And it was perhaps the last number that was most impressive.

During OU's narrow escape from Texas A&M's upset bid at Kyle Field, Peterson struggled against a stout defense revved to stop him. And when in the fourth quarter he left the game and headed to the locker room, his dislocated left shoulder dangling,

"In certain situations, I think he kicks it up a gear," says OU running backs coach Cale Gundy. "And I think maybe, deep down inside him, he knows to win these big games."

Photography by Larry Smith

38 Sooner Pride

it appeared Peterson was done.

Instead, he returned to the sideline wearing a brace. And when OU faced a third-and-2 and needed a first down to continue melting the clock, Peterson reentered.

He bulled his way for 4 yards, passing the 100-yard mark along the way. But the important thing was the first down, which he got.

"That was an extremely huge, huge down," Gundy said. "We ran right into a blitz. He made a couple of guys miss and ran through three or four tackles, ran over one guy at the end to get the first down."

There were other moments, though none so dramatic, that declared to the Sooners that Peterson had the character to match his talent. The skills were instantly evident when Peterson arrived at OU last summer for voluntary workouts.

"He walked in, and I wasn't real familiar with him," said OU quarterback Jason White, a sixth-year senior. "I was like, 'Dang, is that a (junior-college) transfer?' Just by the way he was built. If you looked at him, you'd think he's been in college two or three years and worked out in a college strength program.

"Then I saw him run and I knew if he could get the playbook down, he'd help us."

Uh, yeah. After four tune-ups, Peterson declared his presence to the nation in the 12–0 win over Texas. Making the yards more sweet for the Sooners — and more painful for the Longhorns — was this fact: Peterson grew up a Texas fan. Even as he romped to college football stardom in crimson and cream, a Ricky Williams poster remained on his wall back home in Palestine, Texas.

"He always dreamed of playing for Texas when he was a little bitty boy," said Palestine coach Glen Tunstall, who was an assistant when Peterson played. "But little bitty boys grow up to be big boys."

Few grow into big-time talents like Peterson, though. Back home, they'd known he was special since he zigzagged through opponents in youth-league football. College recruiters made a second home of Palestine during Peterson's high-school years.

But OU won out for a couple of reasons. Peterson said Gundy told him during the recruiting process OU would "win games with you or without you."

"That was something that stuck in my head," he said. And sounded good.

"Most people need to hear, 'We need you,'" Peterson said. "I didn't want to hear that. That's not the kind of person I am."

His teammates agreed. Back to last summer, when Peterson arrived at OU for voluntary workouts. Some Sooners expected to meet a cocky kid. Instead?

"He was the complete opposite," said OU center Vince Carter. "He was a pleasant surprise to most of us. ... He came in humble, ready to work hard. He hasn't slacked off since he's been here, hasn't changed at all."

But he's forever changed the standard by which freshman running backs will be judged. ∎

Sooner Pride 39

> "We don't go into any game looking for numbers ... We go in to win."
> – Bob Stoops

Sooners Ground Tech Air Game
Oklahoma 28, Texas Tech 13

Game 4, Oct. 2, 2004
NORMAN, Okla. - Oklahoma coach Bob Stoops had a chance to make an impression on the impressionable voters in the BCS.

Up 28–13 against Texas Tech and deep in Red Raider territory, the Sooners had the opportunity to make it 35–13 with a simple run or two off tackle. Instead Oklahoma, apparently not worried about point spreads, computer rankings and voter impressions, took a knee and took the ho-hum win in the first weekend of Big 12 action at Owen Field.

That win came only after the Sooners brought the vaunted Red Raider passing offense to its knees. The Red Raiders, a team that likes to play pitch, catch and run, moved the ball between the 20s but was only able to net one touchdown against the OU defense.

"They worked the ball a little bit," said OU coach Bob Stoops. "But we kept them out of the end zone on defense and forced some turnovers."

The Sooners needed to get that production out of their defense, because the offense was rather ordinary. Jason White saw his chances for a Heisman repeat suffer with just 151 yards passing. He did find wide receiver Travis Wilson for a couple of scores in the back of the end zone. It was the second game of the young season Wilson had grabbed two touchdown passes.

"It's just a matter of getting him the ball," White said. "He runs every route hard even if he's not getting the ball. He deserves the amount of things he did today."

Another possible deserving recipient of the ball may have been fullback J.D. Runnels. He is asked to block but rarely gets the ball. Against Tech, however, Runnels did get it. He grabbed a swing pass, took it 13 yards and scored in the third quarter.

"That's foreign territory for me," Runnels said of making it into the end zone. "It's always good to be back there. I just need to be a little bit smarter when I do."

Runnels drew a 15-yard penalty for his end zone actions. It was really the most emotion anyone on the Oklahoma offense showed all day. The lethargic effort was enough to beat Tech, but not enough to overwhelm anyone on the national college scene.

"We don't go into any game looking for numbers or looking to put anybody's numbers where they should be," Stoops said. "We go in to win, and Jason (White) operated our offense ... his efficiency and the way he executed it was really solid."

As was Adrian Peterson in the first start of his career. The freshman running back had 146 yards on 24 carries and a touchdown. It was Peterson's fourth straight game with 100 yards or more. Peterson's 61-yard run in the first quarter was the longest by a true

Freshman sensation Adrian Peterson ran over the Texas Tech defense for 146 yards.

Photography by Larry Smith

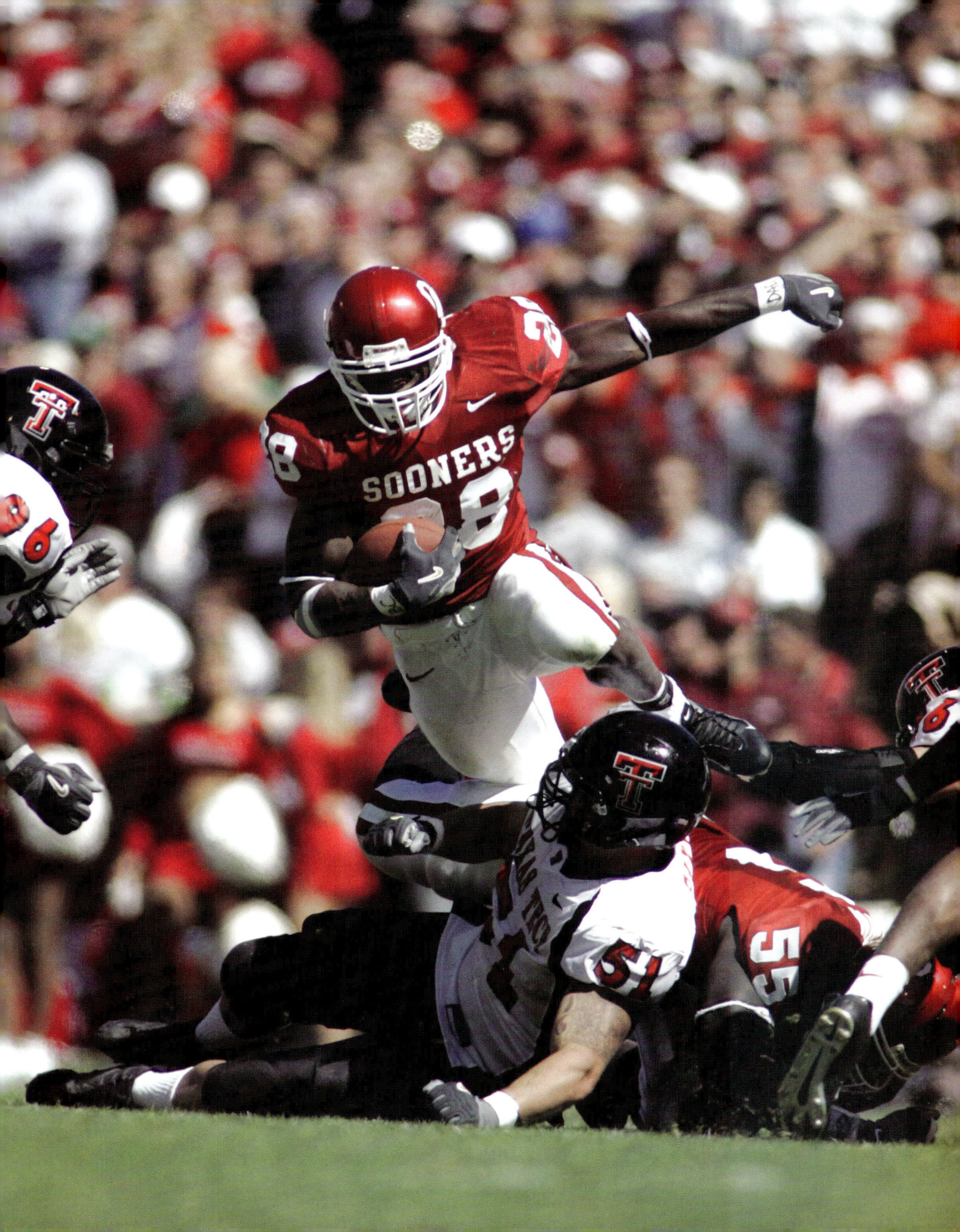
SOONERS
28
51
55

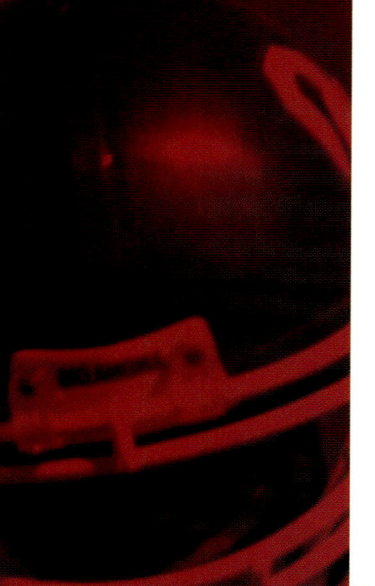

freshman at OU since Renaldo Works went 75 yards in 2000 against Arkansas State.

Peterson also became the first freshman in OU history to rush for 100 or more yards in the first four games of his career. Peterson's early accomplishments forced his name into some Heisman conversations. And some of the people doing the talking were teammates who escorted White through his Heisman season the previous year.

"It's always good having that as the second option," said Runnels about Peterson. "I hate to say that, we're talking about one of the best players in the country and we're saying he is the second option."

White's first option against Tech was Wilson. In the second quarter, Wilson grabbed a 10-yard touchdown to put OU up 14–3 and really put the game out of reach. Wilson's second grab came in the fourth when White was forced to step up, stay up with a tackler on him and hit the receiver across the middle of the end zone.

That pass even impressed the coaches who had thought maybe they had seen everything the senior quarterback had to offer.

"(That play) was one of the best I've seen," OU offensive coordinator Chuck Long said.

"I didn't realize it at the time. How he got out of that and threw that pass I don't know. They had two guys wrapped on him and one guy on his legs."

Tech quarterback Sunny Cumbie had Sooners all over his legs all day as well. Oklahoma had three sacks against Cumbie. That pressure was key in keeping Tech from moving the ball with any consistency.

"(Tech's) offense is frustrating because you hold them and then they get one big one out of the gate on you," said linebacker Lance Mitchell. "It gets frustrating at times but you have to let those plays go. Pretty much you just hold your ground.

"We wanted a goose egg, but we held them under 14 points which we always come out to do as a defense."

Cumbie still managed to complete 36-of-55 passes for 369 yards. But due to the pressure, Cumbie was also picked off three times.

"We still could play better," Stoops said. "We were not as efficient as we as we should've been. We've got some players who are making mistakes on their assignments and that can't continue to happen."

Still, the interceptions fueled a defense that

Travis Wilson scored two TDs for the second time in four games.

Photography by Larry Smith

42 Sooner Pride

coming into the game had yet to grab one.

"We were going to move on anyway, but that gets the monkey off our backs," said safety Brandon Shelby. "All year we've been in the right position to make plays. Tech threw the ball downfield and that gave us the opportunities to make plays."

The defensive line helped out as well.

"Those guys are all around 6'6" and have really long arms," Cumbie said. "I needed to adjust to that and find lanes to throw in."

The Sooners' offense found plenty of lanes. More specific, Peterson, with the help of wide receiver Mark Clayton's downfield blocking, wore a groove in a lane on toss sweeps to the sideline.

"I love the run game," Clayton said. "I like to see Adrian (Peterson) running all around. I like to see him hit that corner and go all the way for 60 yards."

The toss sweep worked so well because of Peterson's ability and his position on the field.

"It allows him to get the ball deep, with a lot of space in front of him and gets him downhill," said offensive coordinator Chuck Long.

From there Peterson's speed was able to take over.

"We've got a big, fast guy and he just gets that edge on them," said tackle Jammal Brown.

Of course, Peterson didn't do it by himself. The offensive line, which was more experienced than Tech's defense, pushed the Red Raiders off the ball and provided lanes for Peterson.

"(The play) would not be there if it wasn't for those guys on the edge," said offensive line coach Kevin Wilson. "He also came into a pretty good deal. He's been a nice huge addition. But he himself has walked into a good deal too."

The deal against Tech was Peterson going anywhere basically any time he wanted.

"We gave him the opportunity to make big plays and he took advantage," said Tech linebacker Mike Smith.

Peterson wasn't the only Sooner to take advantage of the Tech defense. Tashard Choice, a seldom-used running back, had 71 yards on 16 carries.

"Tashard was really strong," Stoops said. "Adrian did an exceptional job early and a good part of the game. Tashard really complemented him. He came in later and ran strong."

stats

Score by Quarters	1	2	3	4	Score	
Texas Tech	0	3	3	7	13	Record: (3-2,1-1)
Oklahoma Sooners	7	7	7	7	28	Record: (4-0,1-0)

Scoring Summary:
1st 07:33 OU - Peterson, Adrian 1 yd run (DiCarlo, Trey kick), 6-78 1:41, TT 0 - OU 7
2nd 12:57 TT - Trlica, Alex 32 yd field goal, 16-84 7:20, TT 3 - OU 7
 08:32 OU - Wilson, Travis 10 yd pass from White, Jason (DiCarlo, Trey kick), 11-73 4:19, TT 3 - OU 14
3rd 09:41 TT - Trlica, Alex 20 yd field goal, 9-77 5:19, TT 6 - OU 14
 04:38 OU - Runnels, J.D. 13 yd pass from White, Jason (DiCarlo, Trey kick), 9-65 4:56, TT 6 - OU 21
4th 10:30 OU - Wilson, Travis 9 yd pass from White, Jason (DiCarlo, Trey kick), 11-85 4:20, TT 6 - OU 28
 04:50 TT - Mack, Johnnie 8 yd run (Trlica, Alex kick), 10-80 3:20, TT 13 - OU 28

	TT	OU
FIRST DOWNS	27	18
RUSHES-YARDS (NET)	24-56	40-221
PASSING YDS (NET)	369	151
Passes Att-Comp-Int	55-36-3	24-15-0
TOTAL OFFENSE PLAYS-YARDS	79-425	64-372
Fumble Returns-Yards	0-0	0-0
Punt Returns-Yards	2-4	1-3
Kickoff Returns-Yards	1-0	3-51
Interception Returns-Yards	0-0	3-42
Punts (Number-Avg)	1-44.0	3-42.3
Fumbles-Lost	1-1	1-0
Penalties-Yards	2-20	7-60
Possession Time	32:23	27:37
Third-Down Conversions	10 of 18	10 of 16
Fourth-Down Conversions	1 of 3	2 of 2
Red-Zone Scores-Chances	3-4	4-6
Sacks By: Number-Yards	0-0	3-18

RUSHING: Texas Tech-Henderson, T. 17-65; Mack, Johnnie 1-8; Filani, Joel 1-0; Glover, N. 1-0; Cumbie, Sonny 4-minus 17. Oklahoma Sooners-Peterson, Adrian 22-146; Choice, Tashard 16-71; White, Jason 2-4.

PASSING: Texas Tech-Cumbie, Sonny 36-55-3-369. Oklahoma Sooners-White, Jason 15-24-0-151.

RECEIVING: Texas Tech-Glover, N. 9-62; Hicks, Jarrett 6-74; Haverty, Trey 5-98; Fuller, Cody 4-44; Henderson, T. 4-10; Olomua, Bristol 3-47; Filani, Joel 2-13; Amendola, Danny 1-13; Bishop, Brian 1-7; Mack, Johnnie 1-1. Oklahoma Sooners-Wilson, Travis 4-64; Clayton, Mark 4-33; Runnels, J.D. 3-21; Jones, Brandon 2-24; Peoples, Will 1-5; Moses, James 1-4.

INTERCEPTIONS: Texas Tech-None. Oklahoma Sooners-Pool, Brodney 2-42; Shelby, Brandon 1-0.

FUMBLES: Texas Tech-Cumbie, Sonny 1-1. Oklahoma Sooners-Peterson, Adrian 1-0.

"This is our house!" – Vince Carter

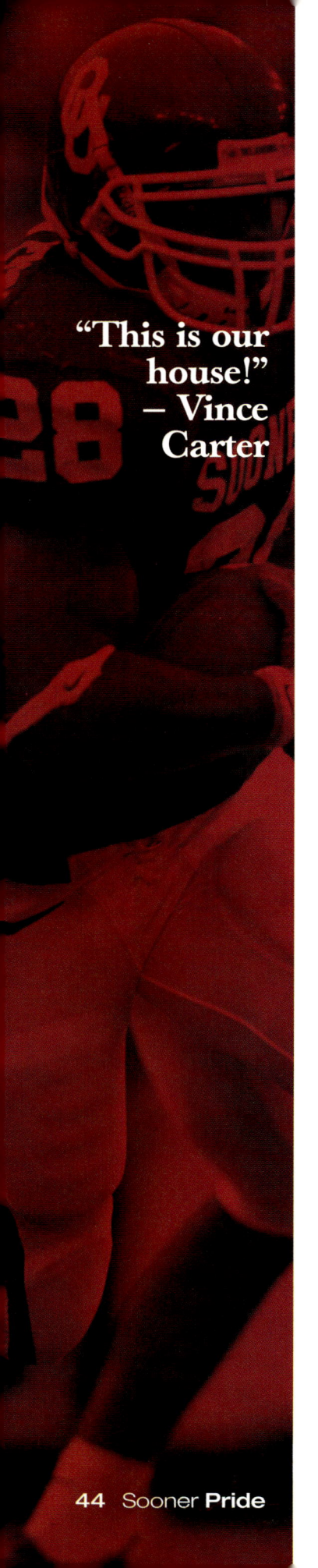

Drive for Five
Oklahoma 12, Texas 0

Game 5, Oct. 9, 2004

DALLAS, Texas – Vince Carter planted the giant, crimson flag at midfield: "This is our house!" he screamed.

The Oklahoma Sooners posed for the familiar team picture, happy scoreboard in the background. And they took turns wearing that golden hat, pulling the rivalry's trophy from its pedestal.

It all made perfect sense. Because by now, it has become, well, old hat.

Oklahoma's 12–0 victory over Texas was the Sooners' fifth straight over their hated rivals.

This one wasn't a rout – not like the 63–14 stunner that started OU's domination way back in 2000, nor the 65–13 whipping applied in 2003. But coming out on top in a good, old-fashioned slobberknocker might have been a more emphatic statement.

"No matter what the score was, we were taking that hat home," junior fullback J.D. Runnels said.

See, this was the one Texas had been waiting for. The Longhorns, who change their approach to Oklahoma annually, had decided the game was really, really important. Since the 2003 debacle, two new assistant coaches had been summoned; soft was out, tough was in.

And the Longhorns were tougher. Afterward, the Sooners admitted so. To a point, anyway.

"They played good," OU senior offensive tackle Jammal Brown said. "But Texas is Texas."

And Oklahoma was Oklahoma.

"Five years in a row, this is sweet," said senior offensive tackle Jammal Brown. "This is the sweetest one. I've never lost to Texas. I'm gonna say it forever."

This time, the difference was a freshman phenom named Adrian Peterson. As 79,587 at the Cotton Bowl and countless others in a national television audience watched, Peterson announced his presence with 225 yards on 32 carries.

"He runs with the utmost confidence," Texas defensive tackle Rod Wright said. "He's not looking for a 5-yard gain. He tries to take it somewhere every time he gets it."

Peterson didn't find the end zone, but that was the only thing he didn't do against the Longhorns – a team he grew up cheering for.

Texas didn't find the end zone, either. Not against OU's defense. Maligned in previous games, the Sooner defenders turned in a superlative effort against the nation's top-ranked rushing attack.

Those early-season questions? On this day, at least, they were like Texas: Pointless.

"We did pretty much what we wanted to do," Carter said.

Which was to say, they won. Again. And grabbed the driver's seat in the Big 12

Tailback Kejuan Jones scored the game's only TD on a six-yard run in the fourth quarter.

Photography by Layne Murdoch

44 Sooner **Pride**

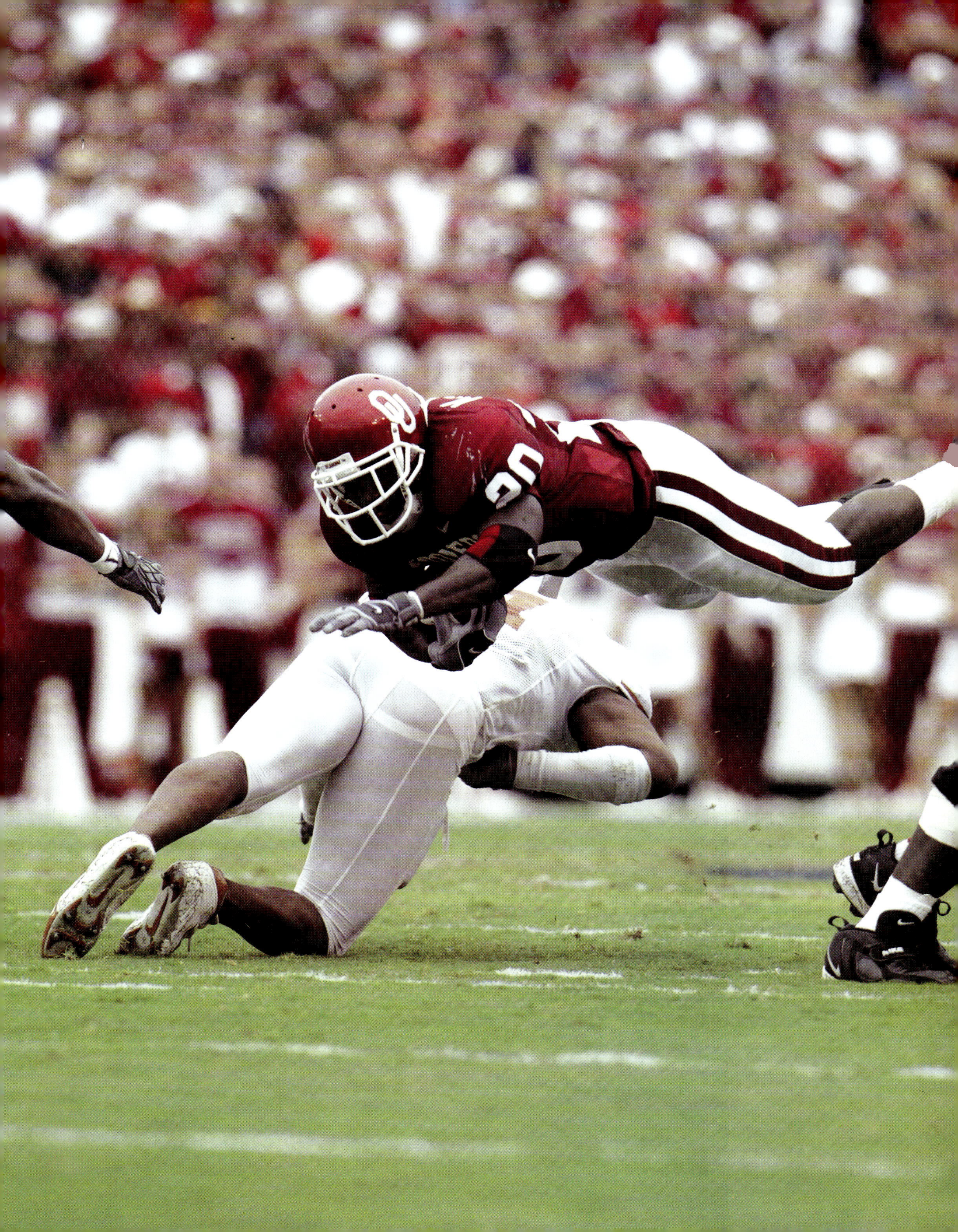

South. Again.

The shutout was the first against Texas in 24 years and 281 games. And the Longhorns' running game, which entered averaging 353.5 yards, managed only 154 on 40 carries. Senior tailback Cedric Benson's Heisman Trophy hopes realistically died in the Cotton Bowl, too, after he managed just 92 yards on 23 carries — 94 yards beneath his nation-leading average.

"Running the football was their bread and butter," OU co-defensive coordinator Brent Venables said. "We were going to do everything we could to make sure they didn't run the football."

The biggest problem for Texas was its one-dimensional attack. Vince Young completed just 8-of-23 passes for 86 yards. The Sooners took away the pass with an array of schemes, blitzes and pass pressures they had not used in the first four games: double-cornerback blitzes. Four-linebacker sets. Moving senior defensive end Dan Cody to a standup tackle or linebacker.

"The first few games, we didn't feel like we'd been playing on edge or playing to our capability," Cody said. "We weren't making as many big plays. Giving up yards. Giving up points. This was a great opportunity to showcase what we're capable of."

And yeah, the shutout was special for a unit that had been questioned repeatedly during the early part of the season.

"This was good for us for a lot of reasons," Cody said. "One, winning the game. And two, our confidence in our defense."

Texas' 281-game scoring streak? It was the longest in NCAA Division I-A. Texas failed to score against OU for the first time since 1972. And the Longhorns didn't get near the end zone. Just once did Texas penetrate the OU 20.

On that possession, Young was stripped of the football. OU recovered, killing the threat. On two other possessions when Texas neared field-goal range, OU blitzes resulted in sacks, forcing punts.

"Their backs were against the wall when we got them in a lot of third-and-long situations," Venables said. "Not a whole lot of people are real prolific at converting those third-and-long situations. It all stems from playing great run defense and keeping those

(above) Linebacker Rufus Alexander forced a turnover with this hit on Texas QB Vince Young. *(right)* In his national breakout game, Adrian Peterson rushed for 225 of the Sooners' 301 yards on the ground.

Photography by Layne Murdoch

46 Sooner **Pride**

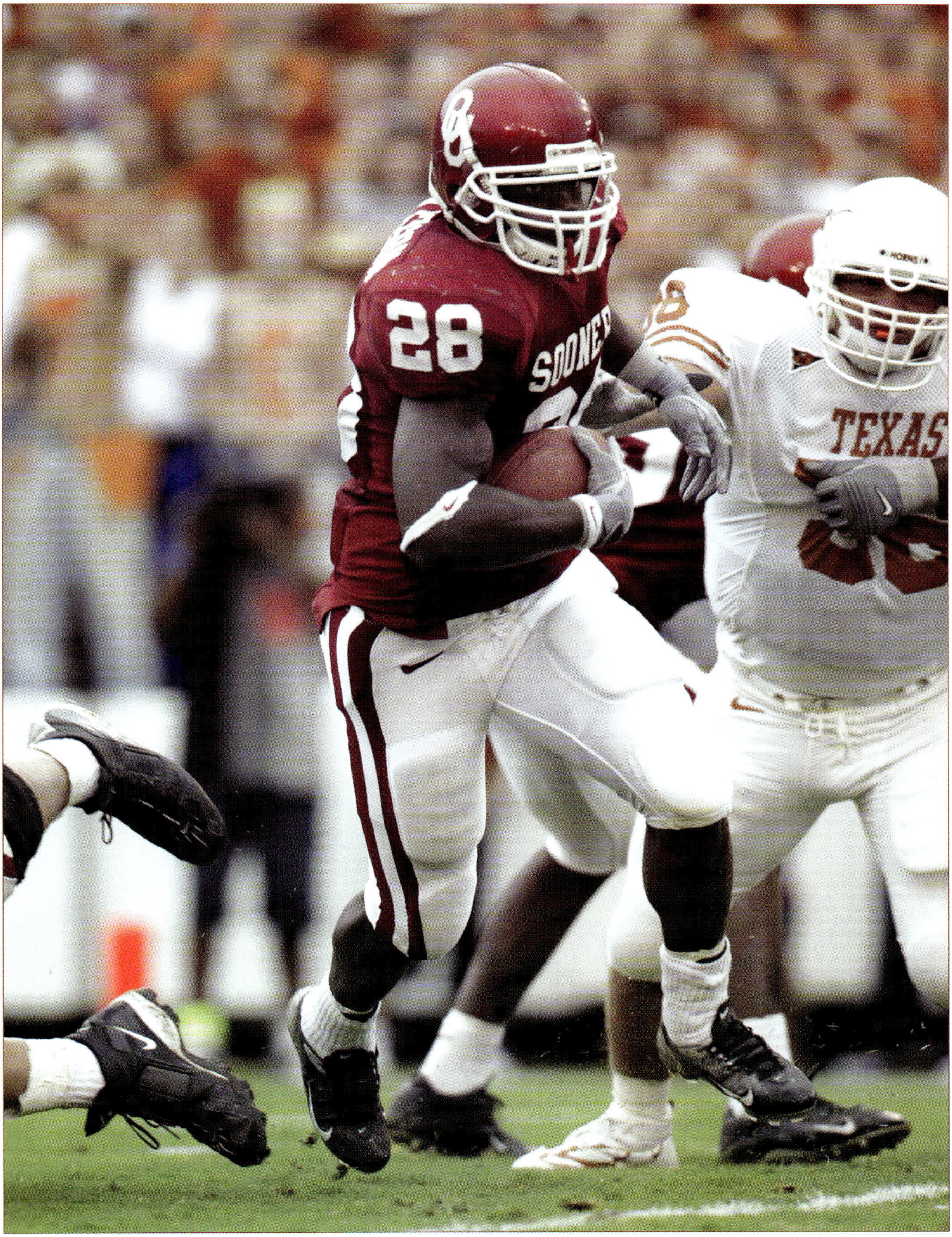
28
SOONER
TEXAS

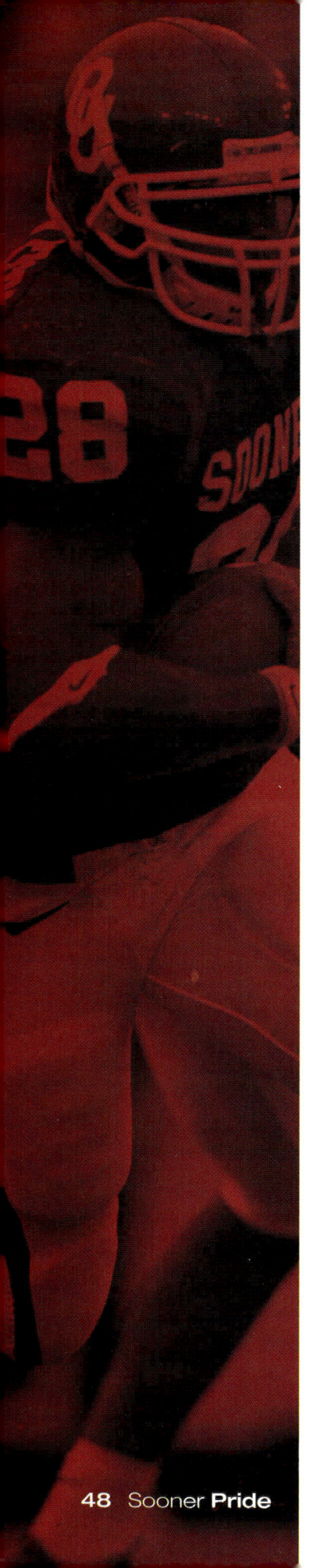

play-action passes to a minimum."

The most important play might have come in the fourth quarter. OU's lead was just 6-0 when Texas had third-and-6 at the OU 32. Venables called for the double-cornerback blitz.

Young turned away from Antonio Perkins – right into Chijioke Onyenegecha. Sack. Threat over.

"You knew the margin of error was none," Venables said. "You knew at any point in time, they could bust one on you."

Instead, Texas' scoring streak was snapped. It was OU's seventh shutout in the Bob Stoops era. But the first six came against creampuffs.

"It's not easy to do against anyone," Stoops said.

And to do it against No. 5 Texas? OU's biggest rival?

"It's pretty special," Stoops said.

The defense helped make up for an offense that moved the football, but struggled to score. Jason White completed 14-of-26 passes for 113 yards, with two interceptions. It was the third-lowest passing output of his career; his only two worse games in terms of production came against Nebraska in 2001 and Alabama in 2002 – games in which he blew out a knee.

"It was an off-day," offensive coordinator Chuck Long said. "They played him well, played our receivers well."

White completed 6-of-9 passes in the second half and was clutch in the clinching fourth-quarter touchdown drive. But the Heisman Trophy winner spent most of the game handing off the football – which, he said, was fine with him.

"The passing game wasn't there that much, so we turned to the run game," White said. "As long as we're winning games, I don't care what we do."

"Jason, as always, managed the game in a great way," coach Bob Stoops said.

Meanwhile, Peterson made up for any passing deficit with a performance that vaulted him squarely into the thick of the Heisman race.

"It's crazy," Brown said. "But look at the numbers. He looks like a Heisman player."

Peterson's season totals, through five games: 771 yards, 119 attempts, six touchdowns. And the performance against Texas was easily his best performance.

"Adrian's gonna be a great player at OU," said Texas coach Mack Brown, who lost a recruiting battle for the player from Palestine, Texas. "We knew that."

He did not start – Kejuan Jones got the nod – because coaches wanted to give him a chance to soak in the atmosphere and calm down.

"We wanted to get him settled in and into the flow of it," said run game coordinator Kevin Wilson.

So Peterson came in on OU's second series. Given the ball near his own end zone, he raced around right end for 44 yards.

"I thought I was going to go all the way," he said.

Some of Peterson's yards came on a play unveiled especially for the Longhorns. After running the toss sweep plenty of times for plenty of yards in earlier games, the Sooners put in a mirror image: 32 Fling featured all the action of a sweep, except the toss went the other way. While blockers – and defenders – raced left, for instance, Peterson took a pitch and raced right.

"We were running a lot of toss plays the first four games and this is a little backdoor off that look," Long said. "They have great speed and they flow hard and we wanted to counter the other way."

OU finished with 301 rushing yards on 52 attempts as Jones added 63 yards.

And that led to this compliment from one of those stunned Longhorns: "They're the same OU team," Wright said. "But they've got a run game now."

It might have been a rout, but for three turnovers and several stalled drives. Trey DiCarlo's 22-yard field goal with 9 seconds left in the first half gave OU a 3-0 halftime lead. DiCarlo added a 26-yarder in the third quarter to make it 6–0.

"We don't mind playing tight, tough games," Stoops said. "We just keep playing hard and stick to what we do."

And eventually, the Sooners found the end zone. An 11-play, 80-yard drive featured Peterson (44 yards, seven carries). But White converted two clutch third downs with completions. Eventually, Jones scored from 6 yards out, pushing OU up 12–0 with eight minutes left.

"We weren't finishing. We had some good drives that we didn't finish," Long said. "But on that drive when we needed it, all the way down the field, that's big. That's the kind of drive that down the road, really helps you out."

It really helped the Sooners out against Texas.

Afterward, the Longhorns praised themselves for playing tough, for not giving up.

"We really thought we would win this game all week," Brown said. "We kept waiting for something to happen."

And Peterson and OU's defense made something happen. Rout or not, the Sooners won. Again.

"Everything isn't always going to be easy," Stoops said after he became the first OU coach since Bud Wilkinson to beat Texas five straight times. "Sometimes, we've made it look easy, and it's not easy. You've got to win a lot of different ways."

And the Sooners have now won a lot of different years. Afterward, junior defensive end Larry Birdine made this promise.

"We're gonna come back next year and go for six."

Red River Domination

The results from Oklahoma's series-record five-game winning streak under Bob Stoops in the Red River Rivalry:

Year	Score
2000	#10 Oklahoma 63, #11 Texas 14
2001	#3 Oklahoma 14, #5 Texas 3
2002	#2 Oklahoma 35, #3 Texas 24
2003	#1 Oklahoma 65, #11 Texas 13
2004	#2 Oklahoma 12, #5 Texas 0

stats

Score by Quarters	1	2	3	4	Score	
Texas	0	0	0	0	0	Record: (4-1,1-1)
Oklahoma Sooners	0	3	3	6	12	Record: (5-0,2-0)

Scoring Summary:
2nd 00:09 OU - DiCarlo, Trey 22 yd field goal, 15-83 6:13, UTEX 0 - OU 3
3rd 09:02 OU - DiCarlo, Trey 26 yd field goal, 10-48 5:33, UTEX 0 - OU 6
4th 08:07 OU - Jones, Kejuan 6 yd run (White, Jason pass failed), 11-80 4:38, UTEX 0 - OU 12

	UTEX	OU
FIRST DOWNS	13	24
RUSHES-YARDS (NET)	40-154	52-301
PASSING YDS (NET)	86	113
Passes Att-Comp-Int	23-8-0	27-14-2
TOTAL OFFENSE PLAYS-YARDS	63-240	79-414
Fumble Returns-Yards	0-0	0-0
Punt Returns-Yards	0-0	3-19
Kickoff Returns-Yards	0-0	1-16
Interception Returns-Yards	2-32	0-0
Punts (Number-Avg)	7-36.9	5-40.2
Fumbles-Lost	3-3	3-1
Penalties-Yards	5-40	5-29
Possession Time	23:58	36:02
Third-Down Conversions	6 of 15	4 of 14
Fourth-Down Conversions	1 of 2	1 of 1
Red-Zone Scores-Chances	0-0	3-5
Sacks By: Number-Yards	0-0	3-20

RUSHING: Texas-Benson, Cedric 23-92; Young, Vince 16-54; Jeffery, Tony 1-8. Oklahoma Sooners-Peterson, Adrian 32-225; Jones, Kejuan 15-63; White, Jason 2-16; Clayton, Mark 1-minus 1; TEAM 2-minus 2.

PASSING: Texas-Young, Vince 8-23-0-86. Oklahoma Sooners-White, Jason 14-26-2-113; TEAM 0-1-0-0.

RECEIVING: Texas-Benson, Cedric 3-33; Sweed, Limas 1-26; Jones, Nate 1-10; Matthews, Will 1-7; Scaife, Bo 1-6; Jeffery, Tony 1-4. Oklahoma Sooners-Wilson, Travis 3-34; Clayton, Mark 3-19; Peoples, Will 2-24; Runnels, J.D. 2-18; Jones, Kejuan 2-4; Jones, Brandon 1-12; Moses, James 1-2.

INTERCEPTIONS: Texas-Huff, Michael 1-14; Johnson, Derric 1-18. Oklahoma Sooners-None.

FUMBLES: Texas-Young, Vince 2-2; Benson, Cedric 1-1. Oklahoma Sooners-Peterson, Adrian 2-0; White, Jason 1-1.

"The pass game was there all day and we had to take advantage of it."
— Jason White

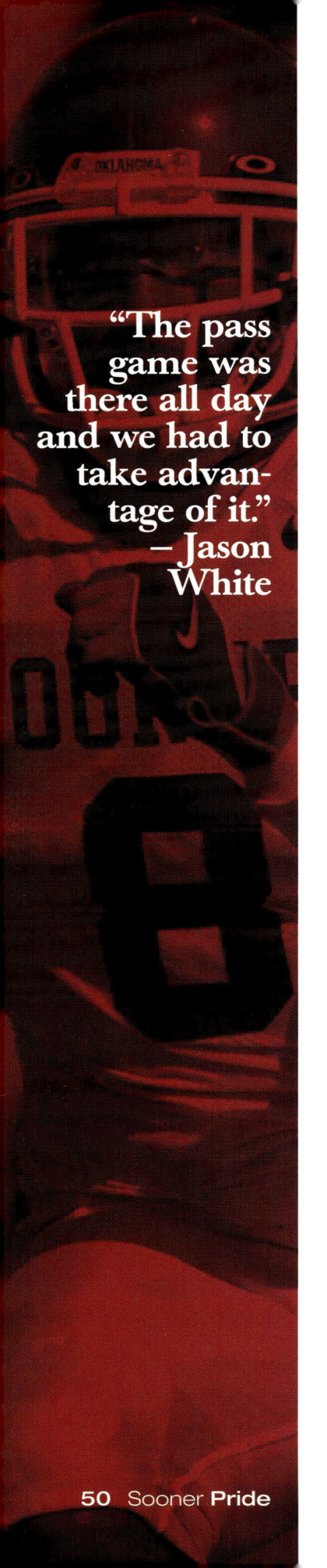

Revenge Is Sweet
Oklahoma 31, Kansas State 21

Game 6, Oct. 16, 2004

MANHATTAN, Kan. - Jason White did it again.

Same team. Same play. Same result

Against Kansas State, White threw an interception that was returned 27 yards for a touchdown. In the 2003 Big 12 title game, White threw an interception that was returned 27 yards for a touchdown. This year, like last, the score put OU behind.

Unlike last year, though, White rallied, threw two touchdowns and helped OU avenge what had been its most embarrassing loss in years with a 31–21 win over the Wildcats in Manhattan, Kan.

"I knew I made a mistake," White said. "But you wanted to make up for it. That pass game was there all day and we had to take advantage of it."

OK, all day may be a slight exaggeration. Nothing was there all day for the Sooners, as they found sledding tough against the Wildcat defense. The Sooners didn't take their first lead until Trey DiCarlo knocked home a 26-yard field goal with three minutes left in the first half.

For most of that first half the Sooners proved to be inept offensively. Oklahoma went three-and-out on its first two possessions and amassed 60 yards in penalties in the game's first 16 minutes.

The defense wasn't immune from poor play either. Kansas State's second scoring drive ate up 79 yards, although 30 of those came courtesy of penalties on the Sooner defense.

"It was probably just adrenaline, running around and trying to make plays out there," said cornerback Eric Bassey.

In all, the Sooners were flagged 10 times for 100 yards.

"We had some mistakes, far too many," Oklahoma coach Bob Stoops said. "We were too aggressive in what we were doing early."

Meanwhile, KSU took advantage and led 14–7. But White found Travis Wilson twice for 55 yards, the latter reception resulting in a touchdown that tied the game.

"We wanted to come out and have the pass be effective as well as the run," Wilson said. "With them crowding the box, it lets the wide receiver get open and make plays."

Running back Adrian Peterson was unable to make any plays in the first half. The freshman who had rushed for more than 100 yards in each of his first five games had 26 at halftime.

"When we got him we tackled well," said KSU coach Bill Snyder. "You saw there were a number of times when we got him flush, wrapped him up with our arms and bent him over backwards.

"Then there were times when he bent us over backwards when we were reaching and grabbing and lunging at him."

Most of those times came in the second half as Peterson started to wear down the Kansas

The OU rushing attack was slowed a bit at Kansas State, but the Sooners still piled up over 400 total yards.

Photography by Laizure Photo

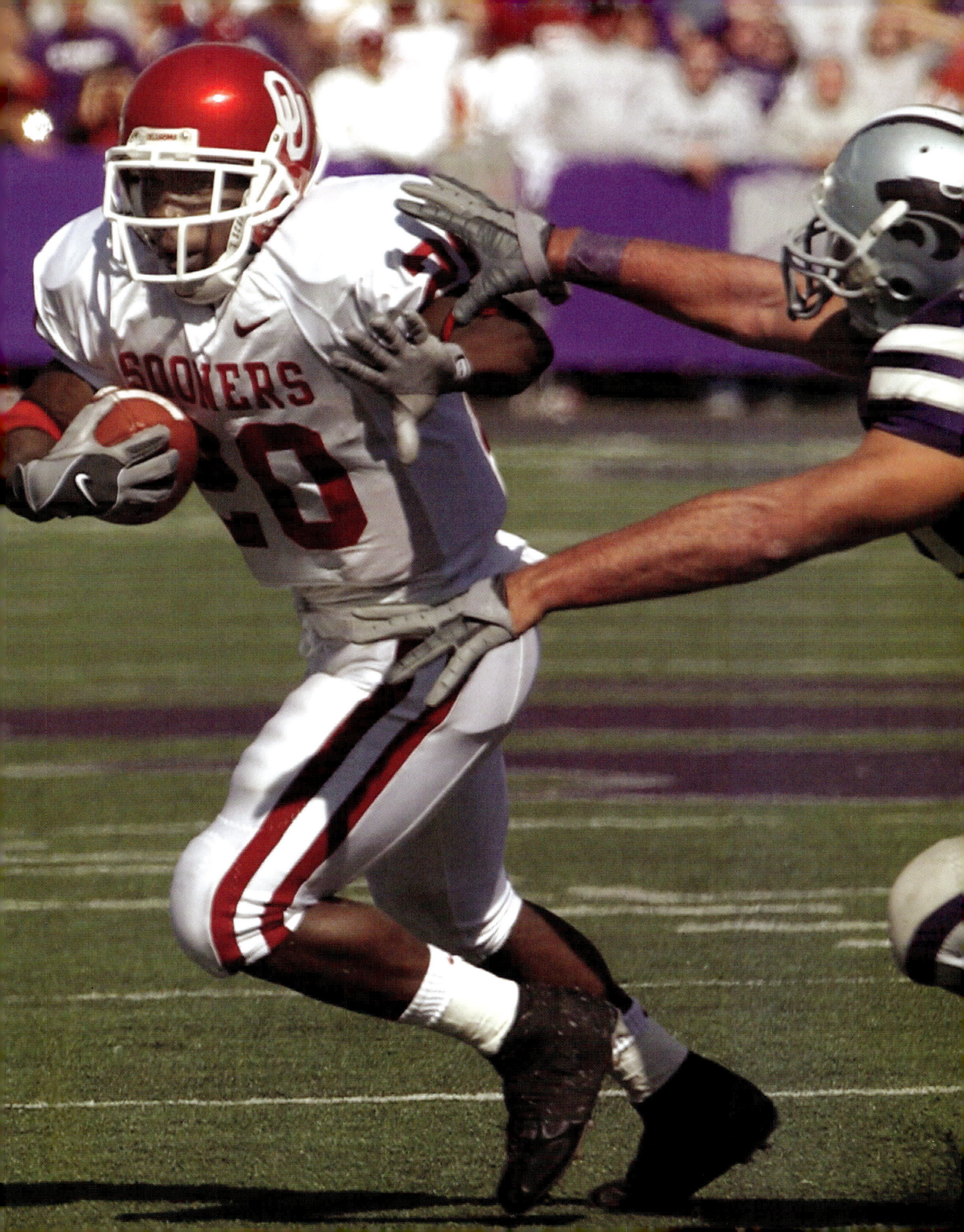
SOONERS
20

State defense. Even when OU trailed 21–17 in the third quarter, the Sooners stuck with Peterson to soften up the defense before White took to the air for the game-winning touchdown pass to Mark Clayton.

"I like the persistence and that our offensive coaches stuck with it," Stoops said. "And in the fourth quarter it made a difference.

"It's not always going to be easy ... usually how you play in the fourth quarter matters," Stoops said. "I love the fact that (Peterson) was really physical and kept playing hard in the fourth quarter. He really made a difference in the fourth quarter."

In the fourth quarter, Peterson simply kept the ball out of the Wildcats' hands. During one stretch he rushed seven times for 46 yards.

"We stayed with it," Peterson said. "Kept pounding them and making plays. We just wanted to go out there and pound it, pound it, pound it all the way to the fourth quarter."

As a result, when the Sooners needed a conversion to keep a drive alive, they were able to keep KSU off-balance because of the running threat of Peterson.

The Sooners, who set the goal of converting 50 percent of third downs, neared that mark with an 8-of-17 day against KSU.

"That's one of the issues that we have had over the course of the year and it comes up and bites us again," said Snyder.

It bit KSU on Oklahoma's go-ahead drive as the Sooners converted on a third-and-2 with a 23-yard pass to fullback J.D. Runnels to keep the drive alive.

"I knew they were expecting Adrian (Peterson) or Kejuan (Jones) over the middle," Runnels said.

Later in that drive the Sooners emptied the backfield on a fourth-and-2 and again converted it.

On the other side Darren Sproles, a one-time Heisman candidate, struggled. He rushed for 34 yards on 13 carries and had a turnover. In the 2003 Big 12 title game, Sproles had torched the Sooners for 235 yards.

One way the Sooners stopped the Wildcats was through sheer confusion.

Oklahoma decided to stand up defensive end Dan Cody and move him around. It was a ploy OU had used a week earlier in a 12–0 shutout of Texas.

"It creates mismatches," said OU co-defensive coordinator Brent Venables. "It's all about their protection."

Against Kansas State, Cody had two sacks and a handful of pressures. Against Texas a week earlier, he also had a tackle for a loss. In the first three games, Cody had just three tackles.

"Maybe early he was a victim of circumstance," Venables said. "He was playing well then but just from a statistical standpoint he wasn't as noticeable."

For Venables, the KSU game was a chance to go up against his former boss in Snyder. Venables knew Snyder's meticulous nature and also knew there would be some flawlessly executed offensive plays that would test the Sooner defense.

"They did some good things we hadn't seen," said Venables.

Rather than rely on Sproles, the Wildcats emptied the backfield and threw the ball at times.

"We were probably a little rattled at first," said defensive back Brandon Shelby.

Photography by Laizure Photo

The confusion was evident as Kansas State took advantage of seam routes, went through the middle for two scores and led 14–7 early in the second quarter.

"Then everything just started calming down for us and we started to come into our own," said Bassey.

After starting 9-of-14 for 124 yards and a touchdown in the first 16 minutes, Kansas State quarterback Dylan Meier was an ineffective 11-of-24 for 118 yards to finish the game. Actually, Meier didn't finish the game. Defensive ends Jonathan Jackson and Larry Birdine met at Meier late in the fourth quarter and sent him to the bench. Allen Webb was thrown into the game and promptly thrown for a loss on a sack.

"Really from the second quarter on we kept them out of the end zone and really started to make some play ourselves in the second half," said Stoops.

And the Sooners were able to vent some frustration over what happened last season when Sproles ran wild.

"Last year he did some things on us that we knew he shouldn't have done," Bassey said. "Our goal going into this game was to stop Sproles."

Safety Brodney Pool said: "We knew if we could take (Sproles) away we'd have a great chance of winning."

The Sooners also changed their blitz packages and began to rattle Meier.

"We had guys slanting directions," Cody said. "We knew coming into the game that they hadn't seen quite a zone blitz package like we had so that's what we tried to put on them today."

"At times we were changing up where we were blitzing from and even when we weren't blitzing," Stoops said. "We tried to keep giving different wrinkles with our pressure to force Meier's hand a little bit and not give him time to hold it."

When it counted, White was able to find Clayton in single coverage for the last two touchdown passes of the game from 15 and eight yards out. Clayton was able to get open in single coverage because the Wildcat defense was focused on stopping Wilson.

"(Wilson's play) did open up Mark and that always will when you have another guy step up," said offensive coordinator Chuck Long. "We feel with Travis' emergence it's going to be hard to double Mark now. They have another weapon to adjust to."

"It was just like a game of checkers, seeing who was going to make the wrong move," Wilson added. "When the pass plays were called, we were able to get open and catch the ball." ■

stats

Score by Quarters	1	2	3	4	Score
Oklahoma	7	10	7	7	31
Kansas State	7	7	7	0	21

Scoring Summary:

1st 09:25 KS - Sproles,Darren 1 yd run (Rheem, Joe kick)
11-59, 4:38, OU 0 - KS 7
01:07 OU - Wilson, Travis 17 yd pass from White, Jason (DiCarlo, Trey kick)
5-61 yards, 2:46, OU 7 - KS 7
2nd 14:07 KS - Figurs,Yamon 38 yd pass from Meier, Dylan (Rheem, Joe kick)
5-79 yards, 2:00, OU 7 - KS 14
10:27 OU - Wilson, Travis 14 yd pass from White, Jason (DiCarlo, Trey kick)
8-80 yards, 3:40, OU 14 - KS 14
03:12 OU - DiCarlo, Trey 26 yd field goal
6-28 yards, 1:54, OU 17 - KS 14
3rd 09:52 KS - Archer, Brandon 27 yd interception return (Rheem,J oe kick)
OU 17 - KS 21
05:25 OU - Clayton, Mark 15 yd pass from White, Jason (DiCarlo, Trey kick)
10-74 yards, 4:27, OU 24 - KS 21
4th 07:06 OU - Clayton, Mark 8 yd pass from White, Jason (DiCarlo, Trey kick)
12-78 yards, 5:12, OU 31 - KS 21

	OU	KS
FIRST DOWNS	23	17
RUSHES-YARDS (NET)	44-149	25-1
PASSING YDS (NET)	256	246
Passes Att-Comp-Int	31-20-1	41-21-0
TOTAL OFFENSE YARDS-YARDS	75-405	66-247
Fumble Returns: Number-Yds	0-0	0-0
Punt returns: Number-Yards	3-30	3-7
Kickoff returns: Number-Yds	3-38	2-42
Interceptions: Number-Yds	0-0	1-27
Punts (Number-Avg)	6-42.0	8-39.4
Fumbles-Los	1-0	3-3
Penalties-Yards	10-100	4-28
Possession Time	31:19	28:41
Third-Down Conversions	8 of 17	4 of 14
Fourth-Down Conversions	1 of 1	0 of 1
Red-Zone Scores-Chances	5-5	1-2
Sacks By: Number-Yards	3-28	1-2

RUSHING: Oklahoma—PETERSON, Adrian 36-130; JONES, Kejuan 4-21; BRADLEY, Mark 1-3; WHITE, Jason 1-minus 2. Kansas State—SPROLES, Darren 13-34; WEBB, Allan 1-minus 8; MEIER, Dyland 10-minus 17.

PASSING: Oklahoma—WHITE, Jason 20-31-1-256. Kansas State—MEIER, Dylan 20-38-0-242; WEBB, Allan 1-3-0-4.

RECEIVING: Oklahoma—WILSON, Travis 5-88; CLAYTON, Mark 5-52; JONES, Brandon 4-27; RUNNELS, J.D. 1-23; MOSES, James 1-9; PETERSON, Adrian 1-6; PEOPLES, Will 1-5. Kansas State—MOREIRA, Jermaine 7-85; FIGURS, Yamon 6-80; MADISON, Tony 4-37; CASEY, Brian 3-29; DENNIS, Davin 1-15.

INTERCEPTIONS: Oklahoma—None. Kansas State—ARCHER, Brandon 1-27.

FUMBLES: Oklahoma—PETERSON, Adrian 1-0. Kansas State—MEIER, Dylan 1-1; TEAM 1-1; CASEY, Brian 1-1.

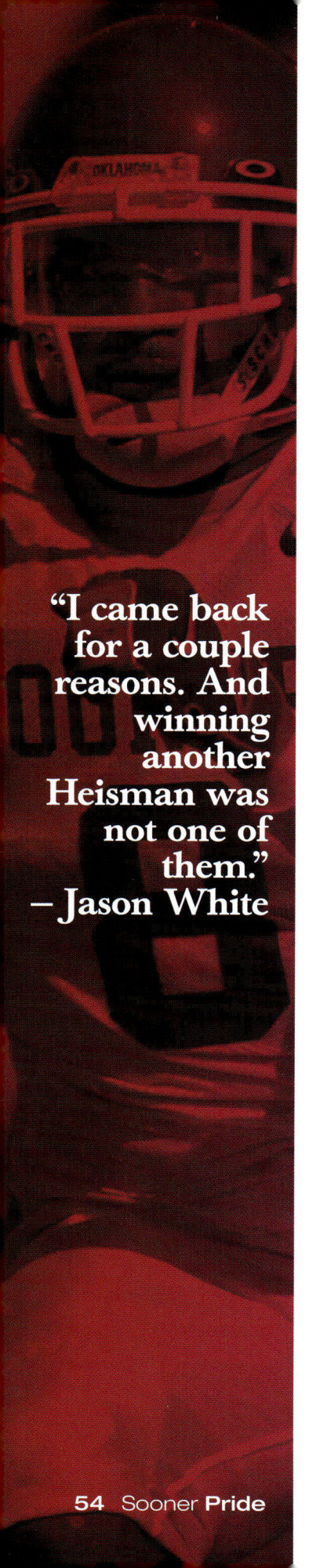

White Gets the Rewards He Really Wants

> "I came back for a couple reasons. And winning another Heisman was not one of them."
> – Jason White

NORMAN, Okla. - He watched, waiting for the winner to be announced. He'd been here before, nervous, wondering if his name would be called.

This time, Jason White knew. He would not win the Heisman Trophy. So it was with detachment that he watched as USC's Matt Leinart accepted the award.

And when it was over, White insisted he was not disappointed.

"I came back for a couple reasons," the quarterback said, referring to his decision to return for a sixth season. "And winning another Heisman was not one of them."

These couple reasons: The Big 12 championship. Another shot at the national championship.

But this was the funny thing. White didn't win the Heisman; he finished third behind Leinart and OU freshman phenom Adrian Peterson. But those championships were testament to an important fact.

White was a better quarterback in 2004.

It started with his health. By the end of 2003, he was banged up after too many hits. He had minor knee surgery during the offseason, and spent time with a wrist and foot in casts.

But even when healthy in 2003, White really wasn't. His knees were more bothersome than anyone let on. He didn't practice on Mondays, in order to rest the knee. And he was slightly more mobile than a "tree blowing in the wind," as run game coordinator Kevin Wilson put it.

But in 2004, White was two years removed from the second knee injury. He would never be mistaken for the young colt who once dashed and darted his way downfield. But he wasn't a statue, either.

And more important, he had continued the natural progression. See, 2004 might have been White's sixth year in school, but it was his second season on the playing field.

The statistics didn't quite measure up in 2004. Though White tossed fewer interceptions, he also passed less. And he was certainly helped by Peterson's arrival.

"He's much improved this year, and that's hard to say with the way he played last year," OU offensive coordinator Chuck Long said. "He's a lot more poised this year, and it showed."

Long's conversations with White went from a coaching monologue to a dialogue. In 2003, White was content to run whatever Long called. In 2004, he had suggestions and input.

"He's just now emerging as that leader that you want," Long said midway through the season. "Last year was terrific, no doubt. But this year, he's seeing more. He's better on the phone (talking with Long in the press box). He's more confident."

Perhaps more important, White's development was evident in his response to adversi-

As masterful as White was during his Heisman campaign, he may have been even better in 2004.

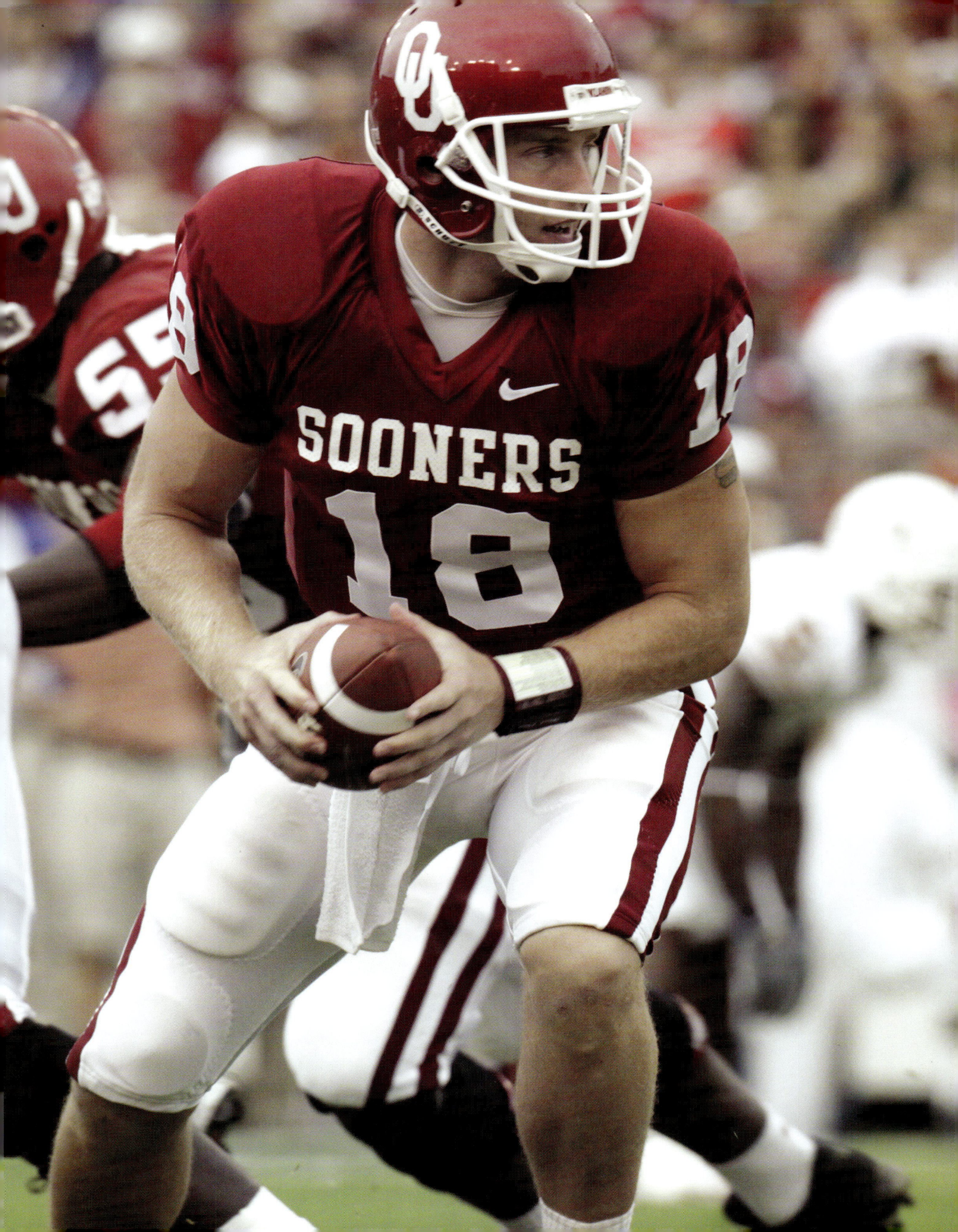
SOONERS
18

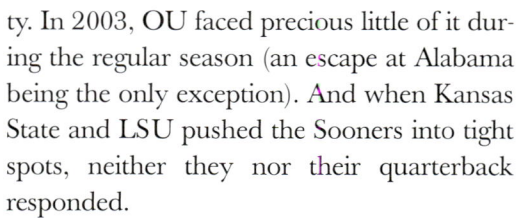

ty. In 2003, OU faced precious little of it during the regular season (an escape at Alabama being the only exception). And when Kansas State and LSU pushed the Sooners into tight spots, neither they nor their quarterback responded.

To be fair, White was injured by then. But a definite difference was obvious in 2004.

"You never knew anything about (how White would respond)," Long said of the 2003 season. "We knew he was tough, mentally tough, but you have to go through things like (2004's adversity)."

If OU wasn't as dominating en route to a perfect regular season, White had more chances to prove himself. And he did. Three times, he led the Sooners back from deficits on the road.

At Kansas State, he tossed an interception that was returned for a third-quarter touchdown, but then led the Sooners on two long touchdown drives to win it. At Oklahoma State, his passing helped the Sooners overcome a first-half deficit.

And at Texas A&M, in perhaps the biggest upset trap of the season, White tossed five touchdown passes — including the 39-yard winner in the fourth quarter.

In all of the above situations, and others less dire, White's teammates said he was in firm control.

While the Sooners might have liked some more breathing room in those victories, they were certainly comforted by the knowledge their quarterback had developed into a clutch performer.

"When the leader of your team is there and he's calm and relaxed and he's telling you everything is going to be all right, it gives you that confidence," said senior offensive tackle Wes Sims.

"He makes plays that matter," coach Bob Stoops said. "You can see that every week."

And the nation did. White completed perhaps his best comeback in a story filled with them. To recap: White was a member of Stoops' first OU recruiting class; he actually played a few snaps in 1999 before a back injury sidelined him.

Then, in 2001, he lost a tight race to replace Josh Heupel as OU's quarterback. But when Nate Hybl was injured against

Mobile, efficient, composed, hungry — White had all the attributes of a championship quarterback in 2004.

56 Sooner Pride

Photography by Larry Smith

Texas, White etched his name in OU lore by driving the Sooners to their only offensive touchdown in a 14–3 win over their archrival.

A couple weeks later, he'd been named the starter, but blew out a knee at Nebraska. Eleven months later, this time the winner of a competition with Hybl, White blew out his other knee.

Some wondered if he'd ever come back. When he did, and when he won the Heisman, it seemed an untoppable comeback story.

"Where he comes from makes it even more special, because you realize the adversity he came through," Stoops said.

Until 2004, when White engineered perhaps his best comeback. And the Heisman was clearly an afterthought; the trophy sat on his parents' mantel in Tuttle.

"After winning the Heisman, not winning the national championship definitely put a damper on everything else," White said. "It would have made it that much better. Don't get me wrong, the Heisman is a great honor.

"But I would much rather have won the national championship."

Don't misunderstand, though. White might not have burned to win a second Heisman, but he was burned by what he heard after winning his first.

Even as he accepted the award, one week after a blowout loss to Kansas State in the Big 12 Championship, there were whispers he was not worthy. And when LSU beat OU in the Sugar Bowl, the reviews came in from all over: White was perhaps the worst Heisman winner ever.

During the summer, White was slighted when media covering the Big 12 selected Kansas State's Darren Sproles as the league's preseason offensive player of the year. The media tabbed White as the preseason all-Big 12 quarterback — but he tied for the honor with Missouri's Brad Smith.

And it wasn't just national perception. Back home in Oklahoma, some fans wondered why White hadn't been replaced, and whether he should even start in 2004.

Take this e-mail White received from a supposed OU fan: "You should give back the Heisman and quit the team. Thank you."

White kept the e-mail and other bits of motivational material. And while his primary goal was to help the Sooners win those championships, he was pleased to learn public opinion had been reversed.

A few days before the Heisman ceremony, White was named winner of the Maxwell Award, also for college football's outstanding player. He was also honored with the Unitas and O'Brien awards as the nation's best quarterback.

"I really was surprised, after the way the season ended last year," White said. "Everybody kind of wrote me off for awards and everything this year."

And yet, his true motivation was clearly evident in the moments after Leinart won the Heisman.

"I've still got what I want right in front of me," White said, an obvious reference to the national championship. "You all know what that is."

Despite his belief Leinart would win, White said he was nervous in the final moments before the announcement.

"When you're up there, you want to win," he said.

But, in the end, he got what he really wanted. ∎

> "Kansas was determined to take away the running game, but White made some great throws."
> — Bob Stoops

Sooners Take Flight vs. Jayhawks
Oklahoma 41, Kansas 10

Game 7, Oct. 23, 2004

NORMAN, Okla. - Oklahoma, which was becoming a cloud-of-dust-type team, decided to take a trip back in time against Kansas.

Sooner quarterback Jason White threw for 389 yards, tossing touchdown passes of 69, 61, 41 and eight yards as Oklahoma rolled over Kansas 41–10 at Owen Field.

"Kansas was determined to take away the running game, but White made some great throws, some great plays and we were just on the verge of making some others," OU coach Bob Stoops said.

The coach on the other sideline, KU's Mark Mangino, used to stand on the Sooner sideline running the offense. But on this day, feelings were not spared as Mangino's Jayhawk defense became just more grist for the OU offensive mill. The KU coach was caught between a rock and hard place trying to decide what to stop, how to stop it and when to wave the white flag.

"Our defense played good, tough football," Mangino said. "We did a good job in the first half. But we were giving up some big plays that hurt us a little bit. And when it got to the fourth quarter we just left our defense out there too long. We're not that deep."

Oklahoma, quite simply, is. But the Sooners didn't need to use that depth at running back. Instead they just kept calling the same number over and over again – 28.

Freshman Adrian Peterson, who needed 99 yards to tie Emmitt Smith and Marshall Faulk as the freshman to gain 1,000 yards the quickest, had 126 on 22 carries.

As Mangino said, KU's defense didn't make those yards easy for Peterson. All but 23 of them came in the fourth quarter, when the Jayhawks were riddled with injuries and sucking air.

"They played very structured and they've made great improvement," Stoops said.

Not enough improvement to stop OU's dual-threat offense, however. White was able to pick and choose his spots and ended up completing 27-of-44 passes.

"He was right on the money toady," said wide receiver Brandon Jones. "But he's been like that all year. He just actually had a chance today. When you have Adrian Peterson back there running the ball, you don't have as many chances. Jason finally had chances today."

Kansas' offense never really had a chance. Not with the way the Oklahoma defense played. Oklahoma's defense had eight pass breakups, four sacks, two interceptions and a fumble recovery for a touchdown from linebacker Lance Mitchell.

"I just picked up the ball and got a great block from Donte (Nicholson) and tried to make a move or two to get into the end zone," Mitchell said. "I was thinking of getting (in the end zone) since I missed out on

Mark Clayton caught five passes for 112 yards and scored on a 61-yard pass.

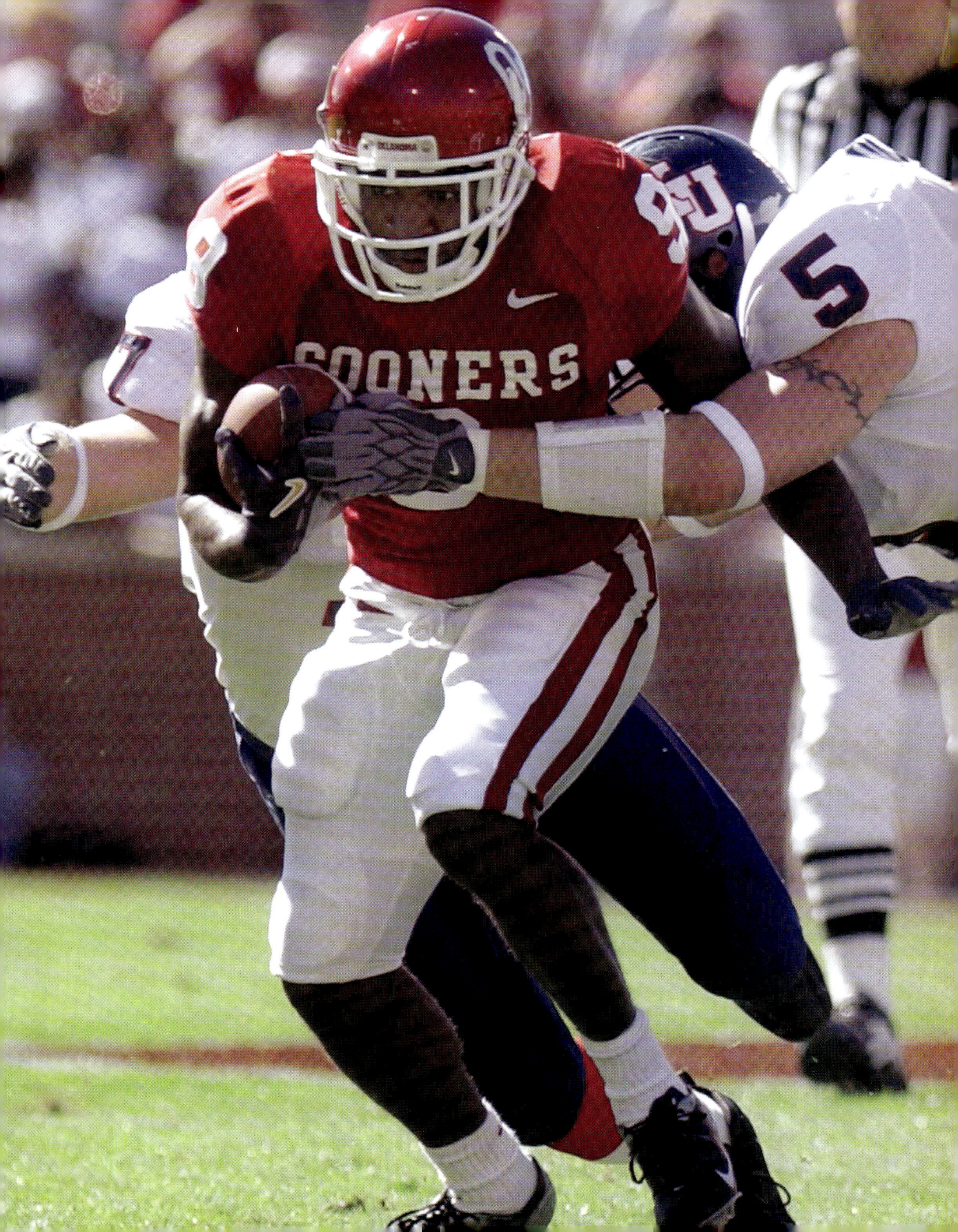
SOONERS
5

one against Tech, so I had to get it back."

It was the 19th turnover the Sooners have returned for a touchdown in the Stoops era. But it was the first defensive score of this season.

"Everything is starting to come together and everybody is starting to play as a team," said linebacker Rufus Alexander, who also had an interception.

The play on defense allowed the offense the comfort to start slow and build up.

"That's what we have to do," said Mitchell. "Sometimes when we're not having enough success on offense we feel like we have to be the backbone. We at least had to keep the score as it was in the first half and keep them out of the end zone."

Well, they didn't exactly keep the Jayhawks out of the end zone. Kansas wide receiver Brandon Rideau got loose for a 78-yard touchdown just 1:29 into the game.

"One of our players just misjudged the ball," said Stoops. "It happens sometimes."

That player was Brodney Pool. The safety tried to jump the route and missed.

"I didn't get a good jam on him but I had the flat anyway," said Chijioke Onyenegecha, who was the cornerback on that side. "And Brodney was coming over the top. That was a bad technical play by me and Brodney should've stayed high."

The Sooners only gave up 106 more passing yards in the final 58:31. On the ground, Kansas netted just 72 yards.

The highlight for the defense and maybe for the game came late, when 300-pound plus defense tackle Lawrence "Moe" Dampeer got an interception and returned it 31 yards. Dampeer, who has the friendly appeal of the late Chris Farley and had a similar body type prior to the season, had been vacillating on whether or not to remain with the Sooners some two months ago. In fact, the freshman went AWOL during fall camp only to return two days later. Still, ever since, Dampeer had been in the doghouse and been subject to some extra conditioning.

"He got a little extra conditioning there," Stoops joked.

Not enough, though, as Dampeer was brought down from behind by offensive tackle Cesar Rodriguez.

"He's a large individual," said co-defensive coordinator Brent Venables. "It was more noticeable than ever. My man, that man is large. When you see him by himself out there on the open field and then you see another large individual run him down,

Defensive tackle Lawrence Dampeer picked off a pass and rumbled for 31 memorable yards before running out of steam.

suck him up ... it was comical."

But it wasn't all sunshine and lollipops for the Sooners. Oklahoma came into the game lacking the same mental attitude it carried into previous contests.

With the ball and a 14–7 lead late in the second quarter, Oklahoma went through a series of ridiculous gaffes that had Barnum and Bailey at the ready with pen and contract.

Wes Sims was called for holding, nullifying a first down. After an 18-yard catch on third-and-17 with 1:12 left, Will Peoples was called for unsportsmanlike conduct for flipping the football at cornerback Charles Gordon.

On third down from the 35, center Vince Carter snapped the football before the rest of the offense was ready; White hurriedly threw the football away to avoid a sack.

On fourth down from the 35, punter Blake Ferguson dropped the snap; the resulting tipped punt gave Kansas possession at the OU 36 with 46 seconds left. That led to Kansas' Johnny Beck putting through a 43-yarder as time expired to pull the Jayhawks within 14–10 at halftime.

"You look at the penalties, the personal fouls, the false starts ... we got to take that out of our game," said Brown. "Mentally we kind of flickered at times. Look at the game film you can see that we played sloppy. Different stuff shows that we were distracted."

The special teams also continued to be a problem. There was a missed field goal, a blocked field, a blocked point after attempt, a bobbled hold on a punt by Ferguson and an anemic punt return unit that only averaged 4.5 yards on six returns.

"Just wasn't disciplined, wasn't solid football overall," Stoops said. "We've got to play smarter. We had a little bit of a lack of discipline, some foolish penalties. We've got to correct that if we're gonna go on and keep improving as a team."

Improving the special teams by no means constitutes wholesale changes. Instead, Stoops said, it's more about being intelligent, particularly when it comes to avoiding blocks on field goals and point after attempts.

"There's no rocket science to that," Stoops said. "It just gets down to having some attitude out there and holding people out. It isn't difficult to do. If the ball hits you in the hands, you have to catch it and punt it. There's not a lot to it." ■

stats

Score by Quarters	1	2	3	4	Score	
Kansas Jayhawks	0	10	0	0	10	Record: (3-4,1-3)
Oklahoma Sooners	0	14	14	13	41	Record: (7-0,4-0)

Scoring Summary:
2nd 14:14 OU - Clayton, Mark 61 yd pass from White, Jason (DiCarlo, Trey kick), 4-91 0:33, KU 0 - OU 7
  13:31 KU - Rideau, Brandon 78 yd pass from Barmann, Adam (Webb, Scott kick), 2-80 0:43, KU 7 - OU 7
  03:26 OU - Wilson, Travis 41 yd pass from White, Jason (DiCarlo, Trey kick), 6-75 2:27, KU 7 - OU 14
  00:00 KU - Beck, Johnny 43 yd field goal, 5-10 0:46, KU 10 - OU 14
3rd 11:36 OU - Jones, Brandon 69 yd pass from White, Jason (DiCarlo, Trey kick), 4-89 1:55, KU 10 - OU 21
  07:42 OU - Mitchell, Lance 28 yd fumble recovery (DiCarlo, Trey kick), , KU 10 - OU 28
4th 09:25 OU - Peterson, Adrian 11 yd run (DiCarlo, Trey kick), 4-27 1:13, KU 10 - OU 35
  00:35 OU - Bradley, Mark 8 yd pass from White, Jason (DiCarlo, Trey kick blockd), 8-47 3:21, KU 10 - OU 41

	KU	OU
FIRST DOWNS	11	23
RUSHES-YARDS (NET)	34-72	31-118
PASSING YDS (NET)	184	389
Passes Att-Comp-Int	35-17-2	44-27-0
TOTAL OFFENSE PLAYS-YARDS	69-256	75-507
Fumble Returns-Yards	0-0	1-28
Punt Returns-Yards	3-6	6-27
Kickoff Returns-Yards	2-42	1-23
Interception Returns-Yards	0-0	2-36
Punts (Number-Avg)	10-45.3	6-36.3
Fumbles-Lost	1-1	2-0
Penalties-Yards	12-109	9-70
Possession Time	30:48	29:12
Third-Down Conversions	7 of 18	6 of 13
Fourth-Down Conversions	0 of 0	0 of 1
Red-Zone Scores-Chances	0-1	2-4
Sacks By: Number-Yards	2-17	4-23

RUSHING: Kansas Jayhawks-Randle, John 11-35; Nwabuisi, Austi 3-16; Green, Clark 4-11; Swanson, Jason 6-10; Cornish, Jon 1-0; Barmann, Adam 7-0; Simmons, Mark 2-0. Oklahoma Sooners-Peterson, Adrian 22-122; Jones, Kejuan 7-14; White, Jason 2-minus 18.

PASSING: Kansas Jayhawks-Barmann, Adam 12-22-2-160; Swanson, Jason 5-13-0-24. Oklahoma Sooners-White, Jason 27-44-0-389.

RECEIVING: Kansas Jayhawks-Rideau, Brandon 4-96; Green, Clark 3-13; Anderson, Lyone 3-12; Simmons, Mark 2-37; Randle, John 2-13; Henry, Marcus 2-8; Heaggans, Gary 1-5. Oklahoma Sooners-Clayton, Mark 5-112; Wilson, Travis 5-81; Jones, Brandon 4-78; Peoples, Will 4-42; Moses, James 3-21; Rankins, Jejuan 2-21; Bradley, Mark 2-21; Runnels, J.D. 1-8; Jones, Kejuan 1-5.

INTERCEPTIONS: Kansas Jayhawks-None. Oklahoma Sooners-Alexander, Rufu 1-5; Dampeer, Lawrence 1-31.

FUMBLES: Kansas Jayhawks-Swanson, Jason 1-1. Oklahoma Sooners-White, Jason 1-0; Peoples, Will 1-0.

"They gave us all we wanted."
— DE Dan Cody

"The Definition of Bedlam"

Oklahoma 38, Oklahoma State 35

Game 8, Oct. 30, 2004

STILLWATER, Okla. – They call it Bedlam for a reason. Mostly, the series has been competitive in other sports. Football has been a lopsided affair, heavily tilted in favor of Oklahoma.

But lately, Oklahoma State has helped redefine the series.

The Oklahoma Sooners were happy to escape – and just barely – with a 38–35 win over Oklahoma State. As a packed house of 48,837 watched at Boone Pickens Stadium, the Cowboys gave the Sooners fits.

"They gave us all we wanted," OU defensive end Dan Cody said.

And more. Victory was not secure until Jason Ricks' 49-yard field goal attempt sailed just wide with 11 seconds left.

"That's the definition of Bedlam," OU quarterback Jason White said. "A close game that comes down to the last few seconds."

The surprising Cowboys, ranked No. 20 in the nation, entertained ESPN's College GameDay crew for the first time. And backed by a revved-up crowd wearing mostly orange, they nearly made the visit really memorable.

It took big days from White (three touchdown passes) and Adrian Peterson (249 yards and several big plays) to keep the Sooners unbeaten.

"These build you," OU coach Bob Stoops said. "We still haven't put it all together. Maybe that's good. We were still strong enough to win."

And he went on to talk about the Sooners' 12–7 win over OSU in Stillwater four years earlier. That would be the 2000 national championship season.

"We went on to finish it out," Stoops said. "A lot of it sets up similarly this year."

Meanwhile, OSU took it hard. The Cowboys weren't claiming any moral victory. Not quite. Coach Les Miles was asked during a postgame interview, "Why do you give (OU) so much trouble?"

"We didn't give them enough trouble!" Miles said. And later in the session, appearing to fight back emotion, Miles said: "My football team … I'll take them around and I'll play any sucker in this country. I like this team. I like the fight in the ballclub. I like the resolve."

But OU liked the outcome. The game, which at times resembled the 2001 and 2002 games – won by OSU – unfolded like a classic middleweight fight, with a flurry of punches by each team. Momentum shifted often, and in a hurry.

"We knew coming in what kind of game it was going to be," said OU senior receiver Mark Bradley, who had three touchdown catches. "It was a dogfight. Oklahoma State is a great team. They will scratch and claw and do whatever it takes to win.

"We just had to come in with a mindset for adversity and finish."

Helped by two special-teams mistakes by the Sooners, OSU grabbed a 14–7 first-half lead. When Mark Clayton, subbing for the injured Antonio Perkins, muffed a punt, OSU recovered and punched in a quick score. Then, OU punter Blake Ferguson dropped a snap (the second straight week he'd done so), and Grant Jones recovered in the end zone for a touch-

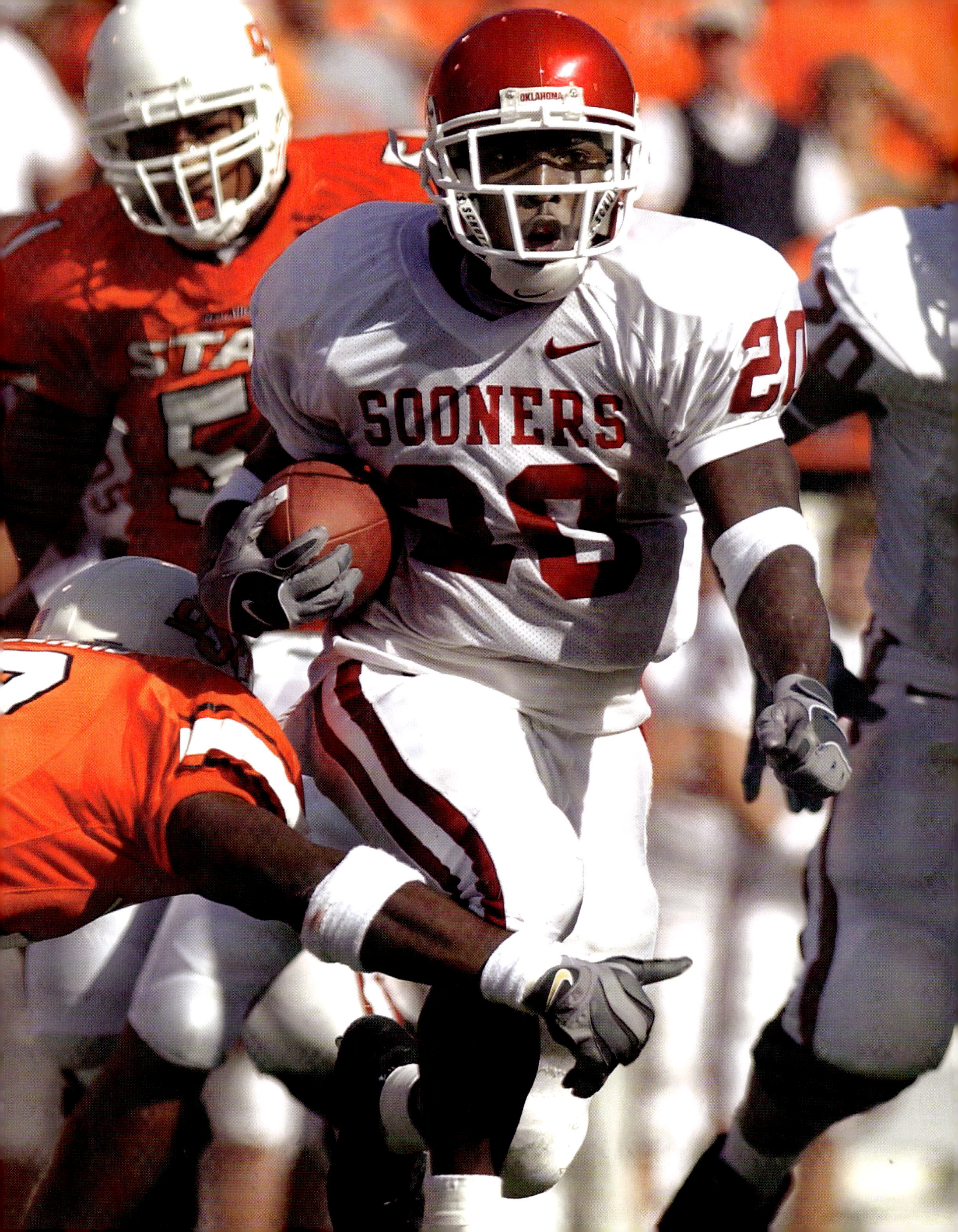
OKLAHOMA
SOONERS
20

down.

But White hit Bradley for three touchdown passes to give OU a 21-14 lead at halftime. Bradley's second touchdown catch came in spectacular fashion. He couldn't handle White's strike, instead deflecting it into the air. But then, Bradley gathered the carom while in full stride, accelerated and raced 72 yards for a score.

"It kind of surprised me," Bradley said. "The ball came out pretty fast. I had a hand in my face at first. It kind of shocked me for a second. But once the ball got cleared, I kind of chased it down and stuck with it."

Bradley's performance was interesting, considering his father, former OU quarterback Danny Bradley, led OU to a 21-20 Bedlam win in 1983. Earlier in the week, the elder Bradley told his son he had dreamed Mark would score "three or four" touchdowns against the Cowboys.

Early in the third quarter, Clayton atoned for his earlier error, returning a punt 50 yards for a touchdown to push OU up 28-14.

"He's not a freshman or a sophomore," OU offensive coordinator Chuck Long said. "He's a guy who's not going to get rattled, and he didn't get rattled."

"I'm not going to jump on Mark," Stoops said. "He's too good of a player."

Enter Donovan Woods. He uncorked the deep passes to push OSU to a touchdown, pulling the Cowboys within seven points.

Peterson answered immediately, bouncing off-tackle, then racing 80 yards to the end zone.

"He still surprises me," senior offensive tackle Jammal Brown said. "Eighty yards. Wow. I don't even think the offensive line blocked that good on that play. He just made a guy miss and ran strong."

And OSU came back strong.

Other than the gimme touchdowns after the special-teams mistakes, OU had held the Cowboys in check in the first half. And standout tailback Vernand Morency was held to 93 yards on 17 carries.

But here was the 2002 déjà vu. Remember OU's last visit to Stillwater, when the Cowboys blitzkrieged the Sooners with a plethora of deep passes?

Woods, Rashaun's younger brother, overcame a slow start — 13 first-half yards — to torment the Sooners. He threw for 194 yards in the second half, mostly on long balls, and helped OSU remain close.

He hit another older brother, D'Juan Woods, for 50, 46 and 32 yards, setting up touchdowns.

"We misjudged their speed a little bit," OU co-defensive coordinator Brent Venables said.

After Peterson's long touchdown run, the Cowboys rolled 87 yards in 11 plays to again pull within seven.

Though Peterson broke free for 56 yards, the Sooners managed only a field goal for a 10-point lead.

And when Donovan Woods connected with D'Juan Woods for 50 yards, setting up another touchdown, OSU cut the lead to 38-35. And the late-moment nail-biting by

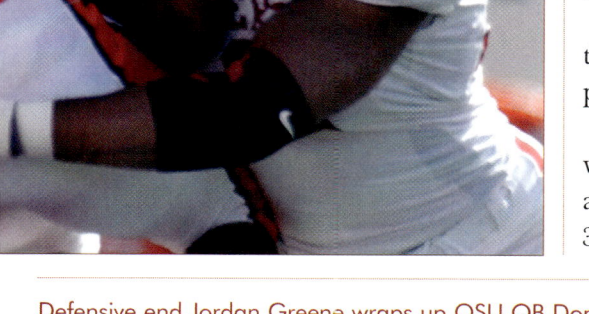

Defensive end Jordan Greene wraps up OSU QB Donovan Woods.

OU fans was set up.

As time ran down, OSU drove. The crowd sensed an upset brewing — shades of 2001 in Norman, maybe, when a freshman quarterback named Josh Fields hit Rashaun Woods with the game-winner in the late moments.

Donovan Woods threw deep, but just overthrew Prentiss Elliott — the football glanced off his fingertips at the goal line, a couple steps beyond OU safety Brodney Pool.

"He was real close to catching it," Pool said.

When the drive stalled, Ricks came on for a 49-yard field-goal attempt. And the Sooners held their collective breath.

"At the end, it kind of sliced like a golf ball," Cody said. "It slid off to the side."

And OU escaped. The Sooners returned home with several thoughts: That Peterson kid could really play. Special-teams mistakes were mounting. And the secondary seemed susceptible to the deep pass.

First, Peterson. The 80-yard touchdown run doubled his previous long scoring run.

"It showed everybody that he does have the breakaway speed in the open field," Long said.

"He's one of the best backs in the nation," OSU safety Jon Holland said.

And the secondary? Remember when Rashaun Woods used to terrorize the Sooners? His brothers did a nice job of reprising the act, leading to questions about the Sooners' secondary.

"A few they threw perfectly, right in the right spot," Stoops said. "A couple of them, we could have been in better position. It's not like for seven other games, we haven't seen (deep passes)."

Co-defensive coordinator and defensive backs coach Bo Pelini agreed.

"Sometimes you get in these games and things snowball on you," Pelini said. "There was nothing magical in what they were doing. Just drop back, run a guy upfield and throw the ball up in the air."

True to form, Stoops found positives, even as questions were raised about his team's ability.

"Last year, when we made everything look so easy, we never were really challenged in those difficult situations," Stoops said. "You've got to win in some tight situations. It's not always going to be easy." ■

stats

Score by Quarters	1	2	3	4	Score
Oklahoma	7	14	14	3	38
Oklahoma State	0	14	14	7	35

Scoring Summary:

1st 03:23 OU - Bradley, Mark 4 yd pass from White, Jason (DiCarlo, Trey kick)
8-61, 3:54, OU 7 - OS 0
2nd 07:57 OS - Woods, Donovan 3 yd run (Ricks, Jason kick)
2-14, 0:31, OU 7 - OS 7
06:21 OS - Jones, Grant 0 yd fumble recovery (Ricks, Jason kick)
OU 7 - OS 14
04:00 OU - Bradley, Mark 72 yd pass from White, Jason (DiCarlo, Trey kick)
5-87, 2:21, OU 14 - OS 14
00:46 OU - Bradley, Mark 23 yd pass from White, Jason (DiCarlo, Trey kick)
8-59, 1:53, OU 21 - OS 14
3rd 10:40 OU - Clayton, Mark 50 yd punt return (DiCarlo, Trey kick)
OU 28 - OS 14
08:45 OS - Elliott, Prentis 39 yd pass from Woods, Donovan (Ricks, Jason kick)
4-80, 1:55, OU 28 - OS 21
08:33 OU - Peterson, Adrian 80 yd run (DiCarlo, Trey kick)
1-80, 0:12, OU 35 - OS 21
02:53 OS - Morency, Vernand 2 yd run (Ricks, Jason kick)
10-87, 5:40, OU 35 - OS 28
4th 13:32 OU - DiCarlo, Trey 27 yd field goal
12-83, 4:21, OU 38 - OS 28
10:34 OS - Morency, Vernand 4 yd run (Ricks, Jason kick)
7-80, 2:58, OU 38 - OS 35

	OU	OS
FIRST DOWNS	20	17
RUSHES-YARDS (NET)	45-267	41-150
NET YARDS RUSHING	267	150
PASSING YDS (NET)	221	207
Passes-Att-Comp-Int	26-14-0	20-8-0
TOTAL OFFENSE: PLAYS-YARDS	71-488	61-357
Fumble Returns: Number-Yds	0-0	0-0
Punt returns: Number-Yards	3-64	1-5
Kickoff returns: Number-Yds	3-36	3-49
Interceptions: Number-Yds	0-0	0-0
Punts (Number-Avg)	5-47.4	7-45.7
Fumbles-Lost	2-2	0-0
Penalties-Yards	10-77	2-15
Possession Time	31:51	28:09
Third-Down Conversions	8 of 16	5 of 13
Fourth-Down Conversions	1 of 2	0 of 0
Red-Zone Scores-Chances	2-2	3-3
Sacks By: Number-Yards	2-16	1-9

RUSHING: Oklahoma—Peterson, Adrian 33-249; Jones, Kejuan 8-49; White, Jason 2-minus 7. Oklahoma State—Morency, Vernand 17-93; Woods, Donovan 18-41; Shaw, Seymore 3-8; Elliott, Prentiss, 1-8; Crosslin, Julius 1-1; Willis, Shawn 1-0.

PASSING: Oklahoma—White, Jason 14-26-0-221. Oklahoma State— Woods, Donovan 8-20-0-207.

RECEIVING: Oklahoma—Clayton, Mark 5-48; Bradley, Mark 4-128; Jones, Kejuan 2-23; Jones, Brandon 1-11; Peoples, Will 1-10; Peterson, Adrian 1-1. Oklahoma State—Woods, D'Juan 3-128; Elliott, Prentiss 2-49; Morency, Vernand 1-17; Bajema, Billy 1-9; Johnson, Charlie 1-4

FUMBLES: Oklahoma-Clayton, Mark 1-1; TEAM 1-1. Oklahoma State-None.

"We won. That's what it all comes down to. It doesn't matter how you win."
— Tackle Jammal Brown

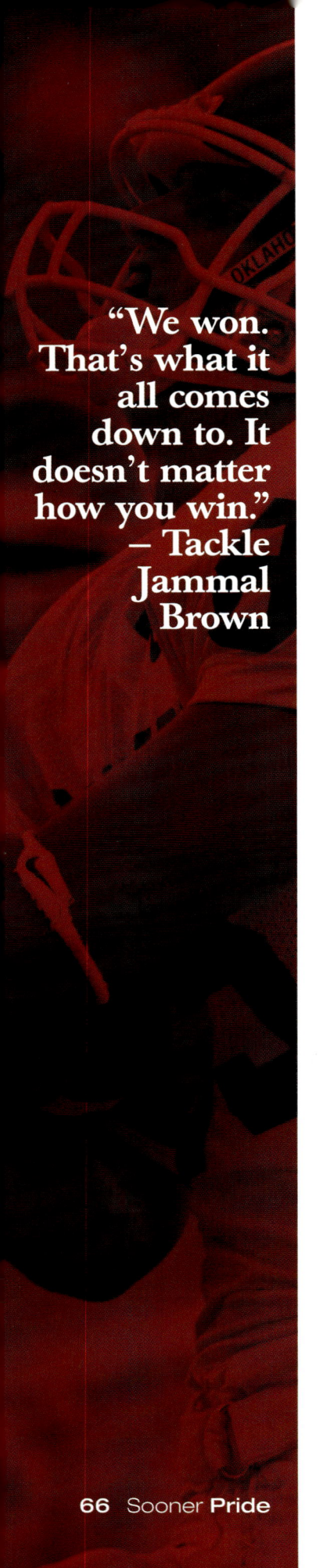

A Little Closer this Time
Oklahoma 42, Texas A&M 35

Game 9, Nov. 6, 2004

COLLEGE STATION, Texas – If there were any doubts left about Jason White's fortitude and ability, he laid them to rest in this one. Just as new doubts arose about Oklahoma's defensive secondary.

White tossed five touchdown passes to lead second-ranked OU to a 42–35 win over No. 22 Texas A&M. The Sooners, who had made headlines in 2003 with a 77–0 thrashing of the Aggies, escaped an upset trap at Kyle Field.

"We were very fortunate," coach Bob Stoops said.

77–0? Not quite.

But, "We won," senior offensive tackle Jammal Brown said. "That's what it all comes down to. It doesn't matter how you win."

At least, not on this day. As 81,125 watched, the Sooners overcame a 14–point, first-half deficit. White, who had attended his grandfather's funeral earlier in the week, tied a career high with the touchdown passes. And again, he came through in pressure situations as OU moved to 9–0 overall and 6–0 in the Big 12.

"He makes plays that matter," said Stoops of White. "You can see it every week."

Other developments weren't as encouraging. For the second straight week, OU's secondary was burned. This time, it was by Texas A&M's Reggie McNeal, who threw for 159 yards and two touchdowns in the first half and pushed the Aggies to a 14–0 early lead. And the Aggies scored touchdowns on a fake punt (71 yards) and a fake field goal.

"There will be plenty to criticize," Stoops said. "But in the end, I'm smart enough to recognize all that we overcame down here in this atmosphere and still came away with a victory. Which makes me proud of my team."

Maybe, the close shave should have been expected.

This was the game the Aggies had pointed to for a year. The fantastic numbers – 77–to–0 – had been burned into their memory banks, fueling them throughout the offseason.

"Seventy-seven nothing," Texas A&M receiver Terrence Murphy told his teammates. "Remember what it felt like."

And afterward, after two desperation passes to tie the game fell incomplete into the end zone, the Aggies claimed no moral victory. They believed they should have won.

"I think (the players) respect Oklahoma a great deal," Texas A&M coach Dennis Franchione said. "But they certainly felt like they could beat Oklahoma. And you saw, they played that way."

During the week before the game, the Sooners insisted they weren't thinking of 77–0, that they understood a different team awaited them.

Adrian Peterson leaps over an A&M defender on his way to yet another 100-yard game.

Photography by Bruce Schwartzman

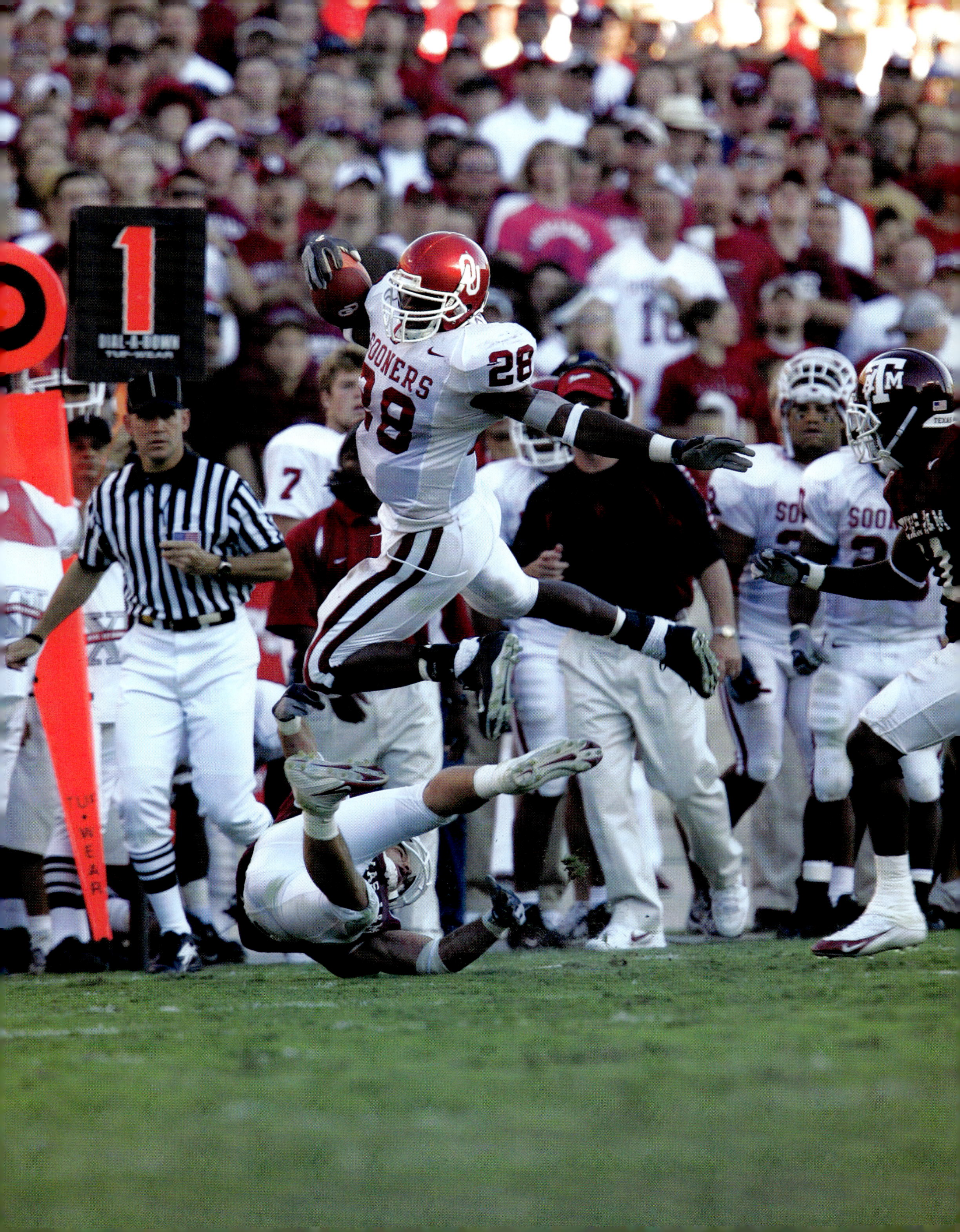
1
DIAL-A-DOWN
28

"We know they're going to come at us," senior linebacker Lance Mitchell said. "We've got to prepare like it's our last game."

It almost became OU's first loss.

McNeal's early success against OU's secondary prompted a desperation move. The plan for true freshman cornerback Marcus Walker had been to redshirt, but that all changed in the ninth game. He replaced corner Eric Bassey after A&M's second touchdown pass.

Strangely, Texas A&M didn't appear to target Walker. But maybe, the Aggies wouldn't have been successful, anyway. After Walker entered the game, the secondary solidified a bit.

"We knew the piano was on our back and we had to lift it off," said junior cornerback Chijioke Onyenegecha.

Onyenegecha was burned on a first-half touchdown pass. But he atoned for the mistake when he forced a fumble on Texas A&M's first play of the second half. The Sooners quickly converted it for a touchdown.

Walker had been pressing coaches to play for several weeks. He'd been practicing with the varsity in case he was needed. And his play against Texas A&M was the first step in shoring up the shaky secondary in the last few games of the season.

"It wasn't just Eric," said co-defensive coordinator Bo Pelini, who also coaches the secondary. "We just needed a shakeup. It was more mental than physical, the things that happened to us."

Another potential disaster turned out to not be such a big deal.

Freshman tailback Adrian Peterson suffered a dislocated left shoulder midway through the fourth quarter — the same shoulder he injured during preseason practices. But after a trip to the locker room, where medical personnel popped the shoulder back into place, he returned to the sideline.

Wearing a brace, Peterson returned to action for one key play. A four-yard run pushed Peterson over 100 yards; he finished with 101 on 29 carries. But that wasn't the reason he was in the game.

"We needed his power in there," offensive coordinator Chuck Long said. "We certainly don't want to put somebody in harm's way. If we get the call from the doctors or the trainer that he can't go, then we won't do that. He was OK to play."

And OU desperately needed him. It was third-and-2; OU led by a touchdown and

The OU defense gave up close to 500 yards but stopped the Aggies when it mattered most.

Photography by Bruce Schwartzman

Sooner **Glory** 69

was trying to run out the clock.

"I felt better," Peterson said. "The coaches make the calls, and they did. I just go out there and run. And the offensive line did a great job opening the hole for me."

For much of the day, there weren't many holes. Peterson averaged 3.5 yards per carry, the lowest of the season. The Aggies' plan was to push Peterson ever farther to the outside, toward the sidelines. Mostly, it worked.

"They did a nice job of stringing him out to try and keep him on the edge," Long said. "I think at times he may have strung it out himself too long instead of just sticking it up in there.

"It was a tough 100 yards."

And on his last carry, with a painful shoulder, he might have drained enough clock to provide victory.

"Every game, I gain respect for Adrian in some other way," White said.

OU took advantage of Texas A&M turnovers to grab a 35–28 lead in the third quarter. But after OU knocked McNeal out of the game in the third quarter, backup Ty Branyon led the Aggies downfield. A fake field goal became a 4-yard touchdown pass, tying the game at 35–35 with 10:08 left.

Enter White and his weekly heroics. He moved the Sooners 80 yards in 12 plays. And the clinching touchdown came on a mistake.

With the game still tied at 35–35 midway through the fourth quarter, OU faced third-and-10 from the Texas A&M 39. Senior receiver Mark Bradley was supposed to run a fade. But when White looked for him, Bradley wasn't there.

White clicked through the rest of his reads and, when the pocket began to collapse, bolted forward as if to run. Then, he spotted Bradley in the middle of the field.

"The corner wasn't going to let me run the (fade) route," Bradley said. "I had to do something. I didn't want to take myself out of the play. ... It was a route that wasn't supposed to be there. But I took it.

"It was a reroute."

White pulled up and fired a dart. Bradley caught the football at the 16, spun away from defenders and raced into the end zone.

"He was at the right place at the right time," White said. "He did a great job – even though he messed up."

With 6:43 left, OU led 42–35.

"Give (Bradley) credit for finding a way to make it work," OU receivers coach Darrell Wyatt said. "But he'd better be real happy he found a way to make a big play."

Mark Clayton danced his way to a six-catch, 102-yard game.

Photography by Bruce Schwartzman

Even so, it wasn't over. Peterson's return helped OU milk some of the remaining clock, but the Aggies got the ball back with 69 seconds left — plenty of time for a last gasp.

Two passes fell incomplete in the end zone as time expired. Junior safety Brodney Pool knocked away the first try. The second fell just beyond the fingertips of Aggies receiver Chad Schroeder — who had earlier thrown the touchdown pass on the fake field goal.

It wasn't pretty. And for one week at least, OU lost some crucial points in the AP and ESPN/USA Today polls. But the Sooners had survived and advanced.

"It's a little too early to be talking about that stuff, but that's what championship teams do," junior fullback J.D. Runnels said. "They overcome adversity."

As do championship quarterbacks. For the third time in the 2004 season, White led the Sooners back from a deficit.

"Just another day at the office," White said afterward.

Except even for White, it wasn't. His performance came six days after the death of his grandfather, George White. White had missed parts of two practices while attending the funeral in Missouri.

His father, Ron White, said it had been a rough week for his son.

"It was the first close death we've had to deal with," he said.

Those five touchdown passes tied a school record White shares with Josh Heupel. White did it for the third time; Heupel did it twice. And White also moved into No. 2 position on OU's all-time passing list with 6,847 yards.

"A really courageous performance after the week he's had," Long said.

White was 19-of-35 for 292 yards, and continued an interception-less streak that started against Kansas State. But forget the statistics, as gaudy as they were. It was White's playmaking ability that impressed his coaches and teammates.

Which brought us back to the winning touchdown. Afterward, the Aggies understood what had just happened.

"That's what a Heisman Trophy winner does," Texas A&M cornerback Byron Jones said. "What can you say? That's what he's supposed to do."

And it was what the Sooners said they were supposed to do, too. ■

stats

Score by Quarters	1	2	3	4	Score	
Oklahoma	7	14	14	7	42	Record: (9-0,6-0)
Texas A&M	14	14	0	7	35	Record: (6-3,4-2)

Scoring Summary:

1st 08:57 TA - Murphy, Terrence 18 yd pass from McNeal, Reggie (Pegram, Todd kick), 10-76 3:34, OU 0 - TA 7

04:42 TA - McNeal, Reggie 1 yd run (Pegram, Todd kick), 7-54 3:01, OU 0 - TA 14

00:21 OU - Wilson, Travis 31 yd pass from White, Jason (DiCarlo, Trey kick), 10-81 4:21, OU 7 - TA 14

2nd 13:53 TA - Schroeder, Chad 45 yd pass from McNeal, Reggie (Pegram, Todd kick), 6-82 1:28, OU 7 - TA 21

10:49 OU - Peterson, Adrian 4 yd run (DiCarlo, Trey kick), 7-73 3:04, OU 14 - TA 21

08:48 TA - Taylor, Earvin 71 yd pass from Young, Jacob (Pegram, Todd kick), 4-80 2:01, OU 14 - TA 28

01:09 OU - Finley, Joe Jon 24 yd pass from White, Jason (DiCarlo, Trey kick), 7-69 1:22, OU 21 - TA 28

3rd 14:08 OU - Bradley, Mark 11 yd pass from White, Jason (DiCarlo, Trey kick), 2-10 0:52, OU 28 - TA 28

08:41 OU - Moses, James 2 yd pass from White, Jason (DiCarlo, Trey kick), 1-11 0:09, OU 35 - TA 28

4th 10:08 TA - Thomas, Joey 4 yd pass from Schroeder, Chad (Pegram, Todd kick), 12-80 6:36, OU 35 - TA 35

06:43 OU - Bradley, Mark 39 yd pass from White, Jason (DiCarlo, Trey kick), 8-80 3:25, OU 42 - TA 35

	OU	TA
FIRST DOWNS	26	23
RUSHES-YARDS (NET)	42-141	33-129
PASSING YDS (NET)	292	360
Passes Att-Comp-Int	35-19-0	38-20-1
TOTAL OFFENSE PLAYS-YARDS	77-433	71-489
Fumble Returns-Yards	0-0	0-0
Punt Returns-Yards	3-34	3-20
Kickoff Returns-Yards	4-69	4-49
Interception Returns-Yards	1-32	0-0
Punts (Number-Avg)	6-35.3	5-36.0
Fumbles-Lost	0-0	3-2
Penalties-Yards	6-64	9-69
Possession Time	32:07	27:53
Third-Down Conversions	7 of 16	6 of 13
Fourth-Down Conversions	0 of 1	2 of 2
Red-Zone Scores-Chances	3-4	3-3
Sacks By: Number-Yards	5-25	1-11

RUSHING: Oklahoma-Peterson, Adrian 29-101; Jones, Kejuan 11-38; Bradley, Mark 1-13; White, Jason 1-minus 11. Texas A&M-Lewis, Courtney 9-57; Branyon, Ty 7-38; Murphy, Terrence 2-14; Joseph, Keith 4-12; Carter, Jason 2-6; McNeal, Reggie 9-2.

PASSING: Oklahoma-White, Jason 19-35-0-292. Texas A&M-McNeal, Reggie 11-24-1-213; Branyon, Ty 7-12-0-72; Schroeder, Chad 1-1-0-4; Young, Jacob 1-1-0-71.

RECEIVING: Oklahoma-Clayton, Mark 6-102; Wilson, Travis 5-51; Bradley, Mark 3-59; Moses, James 3-45; Finley, Joe Jon 1-24; Jones, Brandon 1-11. Texas A&M-Carter, Jason 4-68; Taylor, Earvin 3-103; Murphy, Terrence 3-31; Schroeder, Chad 2-63; Riley, Tydrick 2-37; Lewis, Courtney 2-22; Franks, Kerry 2-19; Mobley, DeQawn 1-13; Thomas, Joey 1-4.

INTERCEPTIONS: Oklahoma-Nicholson, Donte 1-32. Texas A&M-None.

FUMBLES: Oklahoma-None. Texas A&M-Murphy, Terrence 2-2; Carter, Jason 1-0.

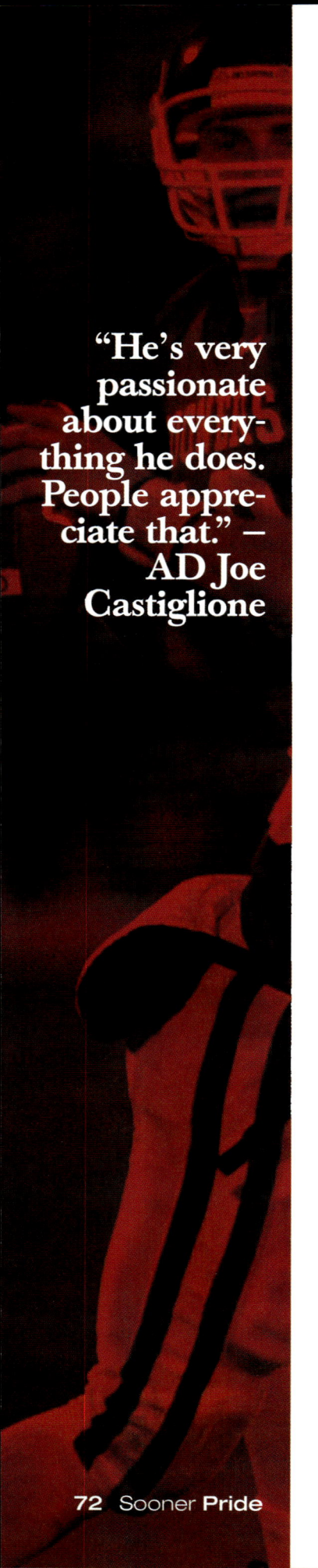

> "He's very passionate about everything he does. People appreciate that." — AD Joe Castiglione

In Bob They Trust
Stoops Has OU Fans Believing Again

NORMAN, Okla. - Around here, Oklahoma coach Bob Stoops has been deified.

Really. As the saying goes, "Bob is God."

Sure, that sentiment may be disturbing on many levels. But it is an accurate assessment of how the many disciples who follow Sooner football feel. For them, winning games is a religious experience. And Stoops — whose winning has also inspired the saying "In Bob we trust" — has won plenty in his time at Oklahoma. Six years. Nearly 70 wins. Throw in three national title game appearances, and what Stoops has done could be considered — warning: another gratuitous religious reference ahead — a revival.

This was, after all, a program that had become flatter than the surrounding landscape for the better part of a decade. While the glory of Barry Switzer's years hadn't been forgotten, nobody on hand was polishing the image or adding to the trophy case either.

In fact, the most lasting image of Oklahoma in the minds of those who were not Sooner zealots was the 1989 Sports Illustrated cover shot that featured one-time quarterback Charles Thompson, a police car and a set of handcuffs.

Stoops changed all that. Not overnight. But almost. He lost five games his first season. He has lost an average of about one game in each of the last five seasons.

"He's a winner," said defensive end Larry Birdine.

Stoops always has been. The Youngstown, Ohio, native grew up the son of a football high school coach. He became a four-year starter at Iowa and took the Hawkeyes to the Rose Bowl. After his career he immediately put himself into coaching. And since 1983, through stints at Iowa, Kent State, Kansas State, Florida and now Oklahoma, Stoops has experienced all of four losing seasons. All came while he was helping build what was then Division I-A's worst program, Kansas State.

During his last four years at KSU it was evident Stoops, then the defensive coordinator, had done the job. The Wildcats were 35–12 and played in three bowl games in that span. A few years later, Stoops had his first national title ring as the defensive coordinator at Florida in 1996.

And in the winter of 1998-99, Stoops got his first shot at being a head coach — in large part because of what he had done, but also because the emotion he exuded when he sat down with Oklahoma athletic director Joe Castiglione.

Castiglione wanted someone with passion. Someone who knew what he wanted, knew how to get it and knew how to motivate others to join him in that journey. Castiglione saw that when he met with Stoops.

"I could tell just in the way he answered his questions," Castiglione said. "He's very

OU took a chance on Stoops, who had no experience as a Division I head coach, and he delivered.

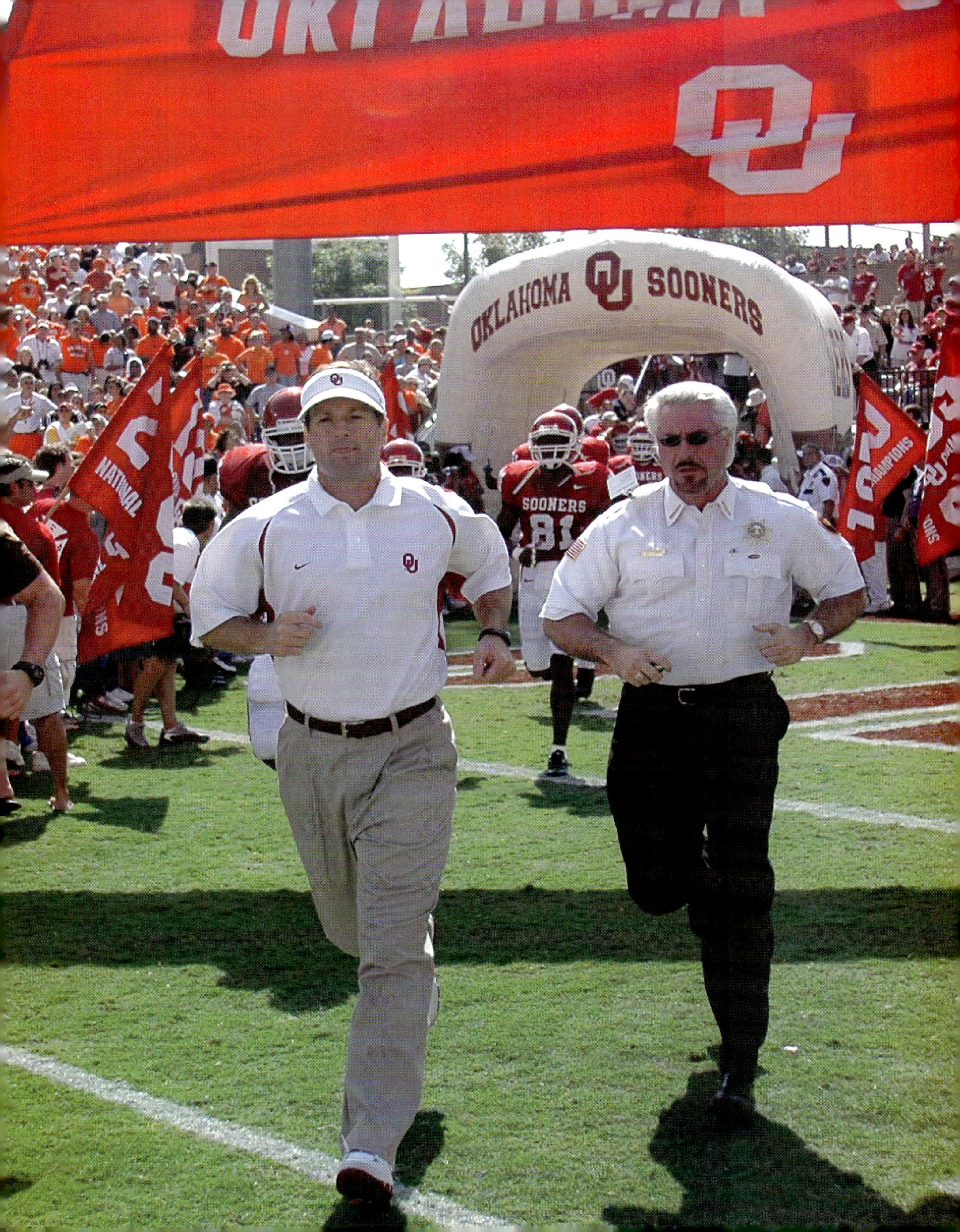
OKLAHOMA OU SOONERS
SOONERS
81
NATIONAL

passionate about everything he does. People appreciate that. It shows that a leader is more than one-dimensional."

Really that passion for OU had manifested years earlier in Stoops' youth. As a kid Stoops used to take a silver marker and paint his cleats. He was an Ohio kid emulating an Oklahoma kid, Sooner running back Joe Washington. Shoot, since the slipper fit back then, maybe everybody shouldn't be surprised it still fits now.

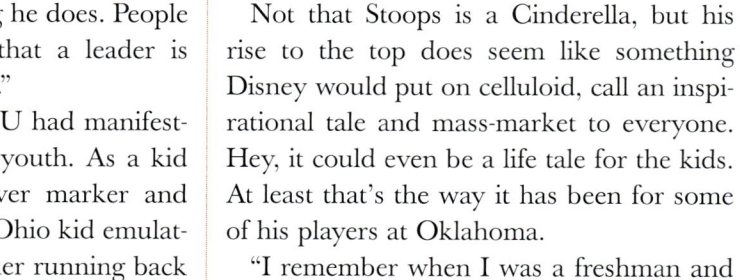

Not that Stoops is a Cinderella, but his rise to the top does seem like something Disney would put on celluloid, call an inspirational tale and mass-market to everyone. Hey, it could even be a life tale for the kids. At least that's the way it has been for some of his players at Oklahoma.

"I remember when I was a freshman and you come down here and things change so fast and you don't understand a lot of what is going on," said Birdine. "He talked to me. Made me understand things."

Through that Birdine began to understand Stoops was more than just a coach on the field.

"He is going to tell you what to do on and off the field to be a great man in life," Birdine said.

And he does it with sometimes-excruciating honesty.

"He's straightforward," said freshman cornerback Marcus Walker. "He tells you just how it is. As a player you respect somebody who is going tell you how it is."

If a player's not getting the job done, Stoops lets him know and will sometimes let him sit and think about why he is not getting it done. In the 2004 season, Stoops twice pulled redshirts late in the season and used those true freshmen to replace veterans.

Walker was thrown into a dicey game at Texas A&M. Walker, who had pestered Stoops all year about playing, helped shut down what had been a potent offense.

In the other instance, Stoops benched 2003 Lou Groza finalist Trey DiCarlo in the last game of the regular season and put in true freshman Garrett Hartley.

It's the way Stoops has managed these situations that has made him successful. He is able to get star players to buy into the team mentality. For instance, Mark Clayton, who'd be a No. 1 receiver on most teams, accepted a diminished role this season and committed himself to block downfield for

Stoops has built the Sooners into the nation's top program in his short tenure in Norman.

Photography by Bruce Schwartzman

running back Adrian Peterson. It wasn't that Clayton's skills had diminished. Rather, the run game gave the Sooners more of an opportunity to win. So the players had to buy into that.

So while Stoops in many ways is old school – disciplined, off-putting with the media, possessing a bunker mentality – he has become a forward thinker in college football. He is more of a businessman who treats his assistant coaches as valued board members, the team as vital employees and fans as stockholders.

"Oklahoma isn't about me," he said. "It's about a team and a program."

And above all, Stoops trusts that team and those in the program.

"He goes above and beyond in regards to giving you autonomy to do your job," said co-defensive coordinator Brent Venables. "It really gives you the freedom to be who you are and be aggressive and confident in that manner without somebody looking over your shoulder all the time."

Stoops came from a program where there was someone looking over his shoulder at all times, Kansas State coach Bill Snyder. Through the years Snyder has become notorious for being overbearing and overworking assistants. It is safe to assume that Stoops learned from that experience; he doesn't run his staff with an iron fist, but instead with an open door.

"He has tremendous respect for the guys he hires," Venables said. "There is no gray area. He would never leave anybody hanging out to dry.

"It's unique in his profession," he continued. "You see a lot of guys who are scapegoats. He calls it like it is."

Because of that, coaches have wanted to work for Stoops.

"Look at some of the people he has hired," Castiglione said.

Many, like offensive coordinator Chuck Long or co-defensive coordinator Bo Pelini, probably could have other, better, jobs, even head coaching positions. But they have remained at OU and worked for Stoops and probably will until the perfect position comes around.

Stoops has lost key assistants like Mike Leach, Mark Mangino and his brother Mike Stoops to head coaching jobs around the country through the years. And he has had trusted his instincts in hiring replacements. To date it has worked out.

"He has the ability to identify strengths and weaknesses in people and see how they fit in the grand

"Oklahoma isn't about me," Stoops says. "It's about a team and a program."

scheme," said Castiglione. "You can see that with the kind of effect he has had on the student athletes. But look at what he has done with his staff. When we've been faced with the task of replacing them he has found someone really special."

So far Castiglione has been able to fend off suitors for Stoops' services. For his part Stoops has continued to contend that he is content at Oklahoma. And as long as Stoops continues to win, the faithful will be content with him, too. ■

> "I feel great about the team and the way we're playing right now." – Bob Stoops

Sooners Bully their Old Rivals
Oklahoma 30, Nebraska 3

Game 10, No. 13, 2004

NORMAN, Okla. – Over the years, Bob Stoops has shown no tendency to run up the score. But in a meeting of old rivals, the Bowl Championship Series' emphasis on the whims of human voters prompted a momentary lapse.

And though it didn't cost Oklahoma a win over Nebraska – hardly; OU won 30–3 at Owen Field – it didn't play well in the world of public opinion.

Leading 30–0 in the final minute, the Sooners were passing the football, looking for one more score to impress those impressionable pollsters. Fittingly, the attempt backfired, and in spectacular fashion.

After OU failed to convert on fourth down with 33 seconds left, Nebraska raced into position for a last-second field goal, averting a shutout.

"I laughed," Stoops said. "It's good for us, that they ended up scoring at the end when we could have took a knee (and run out the clock)."

Stoops said he chose the aggressive tactic because of the Sooners' small cushion in the BCS rankings over Auburn, which earlier in the day had scored an impressive 24–6 win over Georgia. And although Nebraska coach Bill Callahan said he wasn't upset by OU's late attempt to score, Stoops later regretted the move.

"It's unfortunate. What we're doing here at the end of the game, we've never done that," Stoops said. "But if we don't do it, does that come back and haunt you? Then, how do you live with yourself?"

But later, he said: "In hindsight – and not because they scored the field goal – that's wrong."

The final seconds overshadowed a solid thrashing by the Sooners en route to clinching their fourth Big 12 South title in five seasons.

"To be in this position is pleasing," Stoops said. "I feel great about the team and the way we're playing right now."

OU and Nebraska have hooked up for plenty of classics over the years. But there wasn't much luster to this matchup. Nebraska was suffering through its worst season in almost 40 years; the Cornhuskers didn't present much of a challenge.

Despite sluggish play, OU led 23–0 at halftime. Nebraska's West Coast offense, installed by new coach Bill Callahan, exhibited zero scoring punch. Quarterback Joe Dailey attempted just 12 passes – this, one week after he fired 42 in a loss to Iowa State.

Until the final seconds, the most aggressive behavior by a Nebraska offensive player actually occurred during pregame warm-ups, when reserve lineman Darren Delone, heckled by a member of OU's Ruf/Neks spirit group, head-butted the Ruf/Nek and shoved him into a brick wall, knocking out several teeth and sending him to the hospital.

The once-mighty Huskers were held scoreless until the final play of the game.

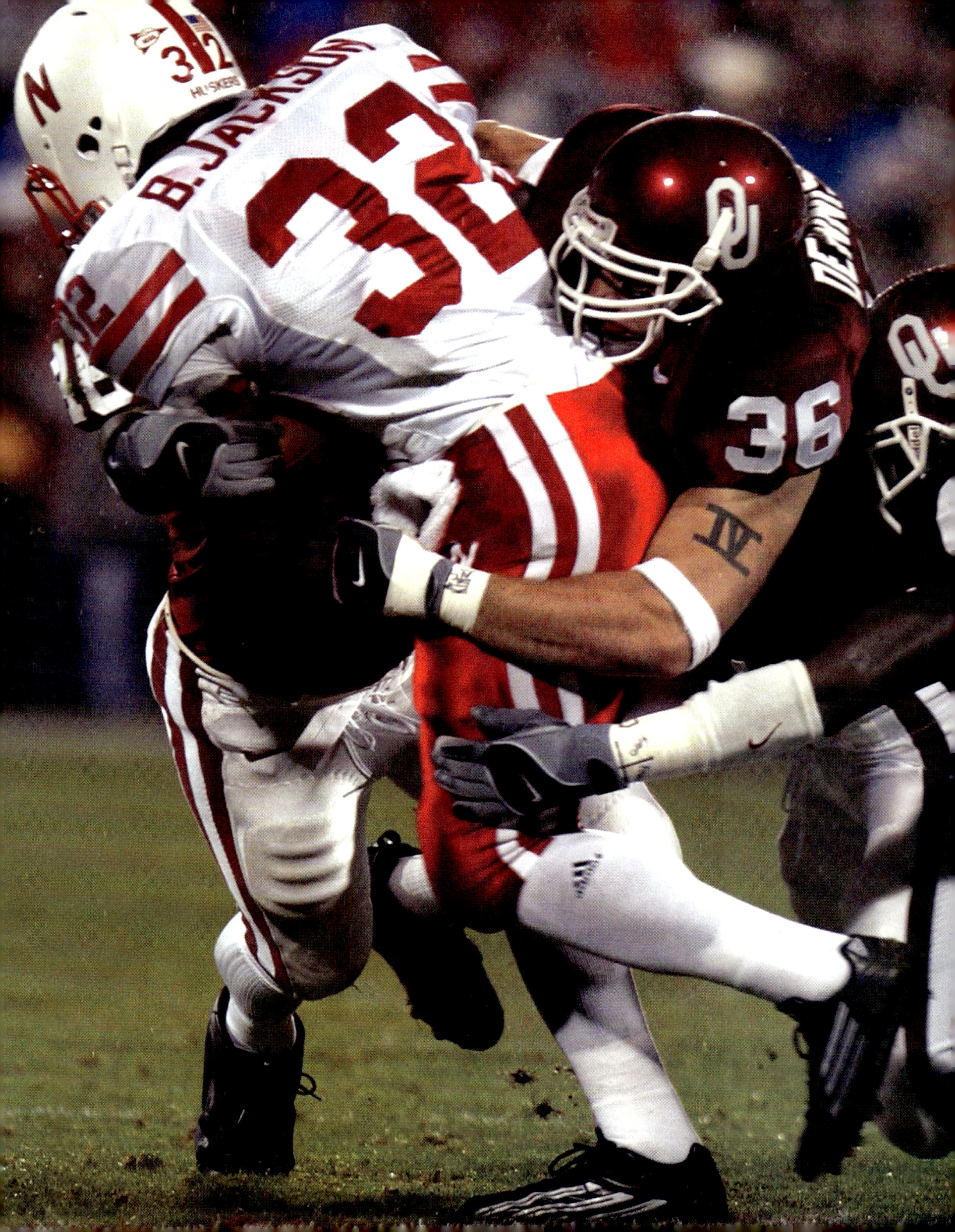
B.JACKSON
32
HUSKERS
36

The most aggressive behavior of all might have come after the game, after those final seconds of what Stoops would later call his own poor sportsmanship, when Callahan yelled an obscenity toward OU fans: "******* hillbillies!" He might have been upset by the fans' boos when the Huskers spiked the football to set up the last-second field goal – strange, considering their cheers moments earlier when OU had tried for a cosmetic score.

"We wanted to score," Callahan said. "We were still trying. We're going to keep trying to score no matter how many seconds are on the clock. I felt compelled to go for the field goal."

And if Callahan was unhappy with the fans, he was impressed with the Sooners, who moved to 10–0.

"The talent is outstanding, skill across the board," Callahan said. "See those plays those guys made tonight? Acrobatic catches, speed, athleticism. ... They've got it all."

Mostly, the game was about Jason White. In his final home game, he set a school record with 18 straight completions. He completed 29-of-35 passes for 383 yards, without an interception. And as he left the field, fans chanted, "One more year! One more year!"

Callahan, who suggested the sixth-year senior had been around for at least nine years, had nothing but compliments for White.

"Their quarterback was phenomenal," the former Oakland Raiders coach said. "He had an all-time streak there with consecutive completions.

"He's very polished, very groomed and very knowledgeable in everything he was doing. He throws with a lot of precision. He's special in every sense."

"He's a great player," Nebraska cornerback Cortney Grixby agreed. "He won it last year, and he's so efficient with his stuff, I'd vote for him (for the Heisman) if I could."

White threw touchdown passes of 13, 4 and 23 yards. His streak of touchdowns without interceptions moved to 19 in five games.

"Jason was just unbelievable," Stoops said. "The guy continues to amaze you, what he's able to do. ... There's no question, through these five games, he's playing better than a year ago."

"He keeps pushing himself," said senior offensive tackle Jammal Brown, White's chief protector. "To him, he's never reached his peak. So good things are going to happen to him."

The final completion in White's 18-completion streak was a 58-yarder to Mark Bradley, setting up a field goal that stretched the lead to 30–0.

White vaulted squarely back into the Heisman Trophy race – even as freshman tailback Adrian Peterson slipped a bit, appearing mortal for the first time in his short but spectacular career.

White completed 29-of-35 pass attempts for 383 yards against the helpless NU defense.

Photography by Laizure Photo

Still nursing the shoulder wounded a week earlier at Texas A&M, Peterson did not start. And he managed 58 yards on just 15 carries, snapping an NCAA freshman-record streak of 100-yard games that had reached nine straight.

"It was fun while it lasted," Peterson said. "We came out with the victory. That's all that matters to me."

Peterson was limited in practice in the week preceding the game. But fitted with a harness, he was available for full duty. Instead, junior Kejuan Jones got the starting nod and rushed for 48 yards and a touchdown on 14 carries.

"He's been playing the first nine games full-speed," said Jones of Peterson. "In college football, there are going to be times when you get banged up.

"Me being the veteran back there, I knew that was going to come. I just had to step up and let him know that, 'Hey, I'm behind you and get healthy because we do need you.'"

"I feel like I performed pretty good when I got in there," Peterson said. "I'm a little sore, but that played no factor."

Nebraska's only offensive success came via the running game. Led by Cory Ross, who had 130 yards on 30 carries, the Huskers rushed for 201 yards on 40 attempts.

Although it appeared to be a play-it-safe-and-get-out-without-humiliation strategy, the Huskers claimed they believed they could have success running directly at the OU defense.

"Obviously, it was going to be tough," Nebraska tight end Dusty Keiser said. " They're a great team. But we felt we could do some things. We worked hard, we played hard, but they were just the better team today."

After White's fourth down pass fell incomplete with 33 seconds left, Nebraska fullback Steve Kriewald rumbled 48 yards.

Dailey spiked the football to stop the clock. And David Dyches nailed a 39-yard field goal as time expired, preventing the Sooners from recording their second shutout of the season.

"We wanted to see that goose egg on the scoreboard," senior linebacker Lance Mitchell said.

Instead, the Sooners left realizing they might have laid an egg. They pondered what factor the misfired scoring attempt might play in their BCS fortunes.

And what else they could have or should have done.

"The BCS is making us think that we're bullies, but we're really not," Jones said. "You don't want to dog a team out, up 30–0 with 30 seconds left. But the way the system is, you've got to score as many points as you can.

"That's what we were trying to do tonight. It's a weird position to be in." ■

stats

Score by Quarters	1	2	3	4	Score	
Nebraska	0	0	0	3	3	Record: (5-5, 3-4)
Oklahoma Sooners	3	20	7	0	30	Record: (10-0, 7-0)

Scoring Summary:
1st 08:16 OU - DiCarlo, Trey 32 yd field goal, 14-68 6:44, NU 0 - OU 3
2nd 10:55 OU - Roberts, Willie 13 yd pass from White, Jason (DiCarlo, Trey kick failed), 11-70 4:31, NU 0 - OU 9
　08:03 OU - Jones, Kejuan 1 yd run (DiCarlo, Trey kick), 2-31 0:24, NU 0 - OU 16
　00:59 OU - Jones, Brandon 4 yd pass from White, Jason (DiCarlo, Trey kick), 9-83 4:03, NU 0 - OU 23
3rd 11:11 OU - Bradley, Mark 23 yd pass from White, Jason (DiCarlo, Trey kick), 5-79 2:12, NU 0 - OU 30
4th 00:00 NU - Dyches, David 39 yd field goal, 4-66 0:33, NU 3 - OU 30

	NU	OU
FIRST DOWNS	13	24
RUSHES-YARDS (NET)	40-201	31-98
PASSING YDS (NET)	73	413
Passes Att-Comp-Int	13-8-1	36-30-0
TOTAL OFFENSE PLAYS-YARDS	53-274	67-511
Fumble Returns-Yards	0-0	0-0
Punt Returns-Yards	0-0	0-0
Kickoff Returns-Yards	2-37	1-14
Interception Returns-Yards	0-0	1-10
Punts (Number-Avg)	6-39.3	2-43.0
Fumbles-Lost	0-0	1-0
Penalties-Yards	7-60	4-45
Possession Time	27:19	32:41
Third-Down Conversions	4 of 11	6 of 12
Fourth-Down Conversions	0 of 1	1 of 2
Red-Zone Scores-Chances	0-1	4-6
Sacks By: Number-Yards	0-0	1-2

RUSHING: Nebraska-Ross,Cory 30-130; Kriewald, Steve 2-51; Jackson, Brandon 5-23; Horne, David 1-minus 1; Dailey, Joe 2-minus 2. Oklahoma Sooners-Peterson, Adrian 15-58; Jones, Kejuan 14-48; White, Jason 2-minus 8.

PASSING: Nebraska-Dailey, Joe 8-12-1-73; Team 0-1-0-0. Oklahoma Sooners-White, Jason 29-35-0-383; Bradley, Mark 1-1-0-30.

RECEIVING: Nebraska-Fluellen, Isaiah 3-22; Ross,Cory 2-29; Keiser, Dusty 1-11; Mulkey, Grant 1-7; Horne, David 1-4. Oklahoma Sooners-Wilson, Travis 9-135; Clayton, Mark 5-61; Bradley, Mark 3-92; Jones, Kejuan 3-40; Runnels, J.D. 3-21; Peoples, Will 2-28; Roberts, Willie 1-13; Rankins, Jejuan 1-10; Moses, James 1-5; Ford, Ataleo 1-4; Jones, Brandon 1-4.

INTERCEPTIONS: Nebraska-None. Oklahoma Sooners-Allen, Gayron 1-10.

FUMBLES: Nebraska-None. Oklahoma Sooners-White, Jason 1-0.

> "It's gratifying. But we realize the biggest prize is still out there."
> – Bob Stoops

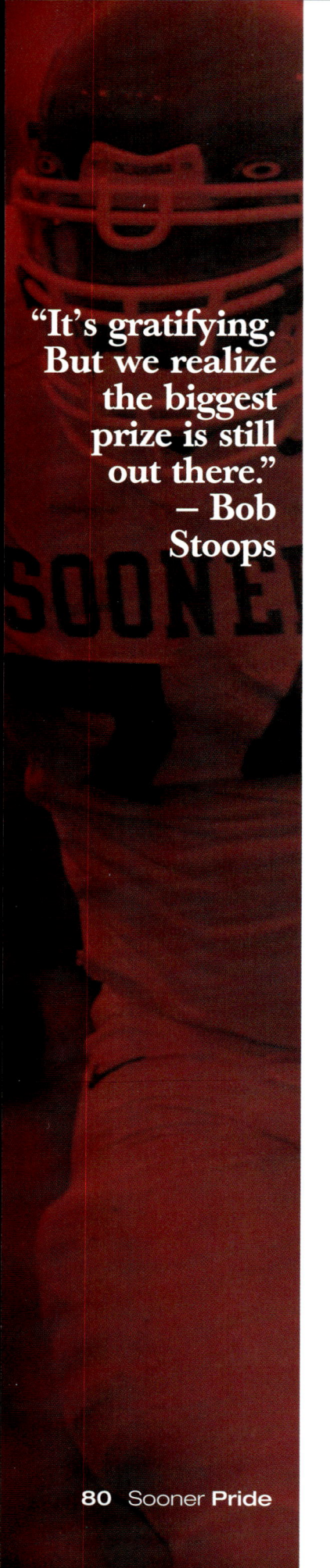

Sportsmanship over Style
Oklahoma 35, Baylor 0

Game 11, Nov. 20, 2004

WACO, Texas – So you wondered, in light of the tight race in the BCS rankings, how Oklahoma could possibly impress anyone with a victory over Baylor. A no-win situation, even with a big win?

Somehow, the Sooners accomplished a cosmetic victory. As 32,182 watched at Floyd Casey Stadium – mostly OU fans – the Sooners chose a different strategy.

As in, they surged to a big lead, then sat on it. No running it up. Not at all.

"I'm comfortable in the fact we chose to run the clock out," OU coach Bob Stoops said.

The context, of course, was the Sooners' 30–3 win over Nebraska the previous week, when OU (and Stoops, mostly) had taken criticism for attempting to tack on a late score. And it was Auburn's game at Alabama, which was played after OU's win over Baylor. The Tigers won, 21–13, but struggled some against a mediocre Crimson Tide club.

The Sooners, of course, had no idea what Auburn might do. But Stoops & Co. realized they needed to win and look good doing so.

Stoops, however, might have gained style points by not letting this game get completely out of hand. OU's reserves played out the final minutes, even though OU probably could have added a couple more touchdowns. Stoops called it a choice of "sportsmanship over BCS points."

OU offensive tackle Jammal Brown said the Sooners had done plenty to impress voters.

"That makes a big statement," Brown said. "Baylor's not an elite team, but 35 to zero. There ain't no way around it."

OU finished its regular season unbeaten for the second straight year. But the Sooners weren't doing too much celebrating. Something about 2003, when they lost in the Big 12 championship and the Sugar Bowl, seemed to prevent that.

"It's gratifying," said Stoops of the perfect season. "But we realize the biggest prize is still out there. Guys are aware of that. There wasn't too much celebration."

OU was sluggish early but revved up late in the second quarter. Meanwhile, the defense was dominant.

Late in the first half, OU held a 7–0 lead – a partial score that, if announced as a halftime score, would certainly reverberate through press boxes filled with impressionable voters.

Jason White had hit just 4-of-13 passes. Junior kicker Trey DiCarlo had missed a 42-yard field goal – his sixth miss in eight attempts. The Sooners were sputtering.

"I don't know what it was," said senior center Vince Carter, a Waco native. "We were just trying to do too much."

Fortunately for the Sooners, they caught a spark in the final three minutes of the first half. White went into the hurry-up offense

The Sooners disposed of the lowly Bears with little difficulty, and a lot of class.

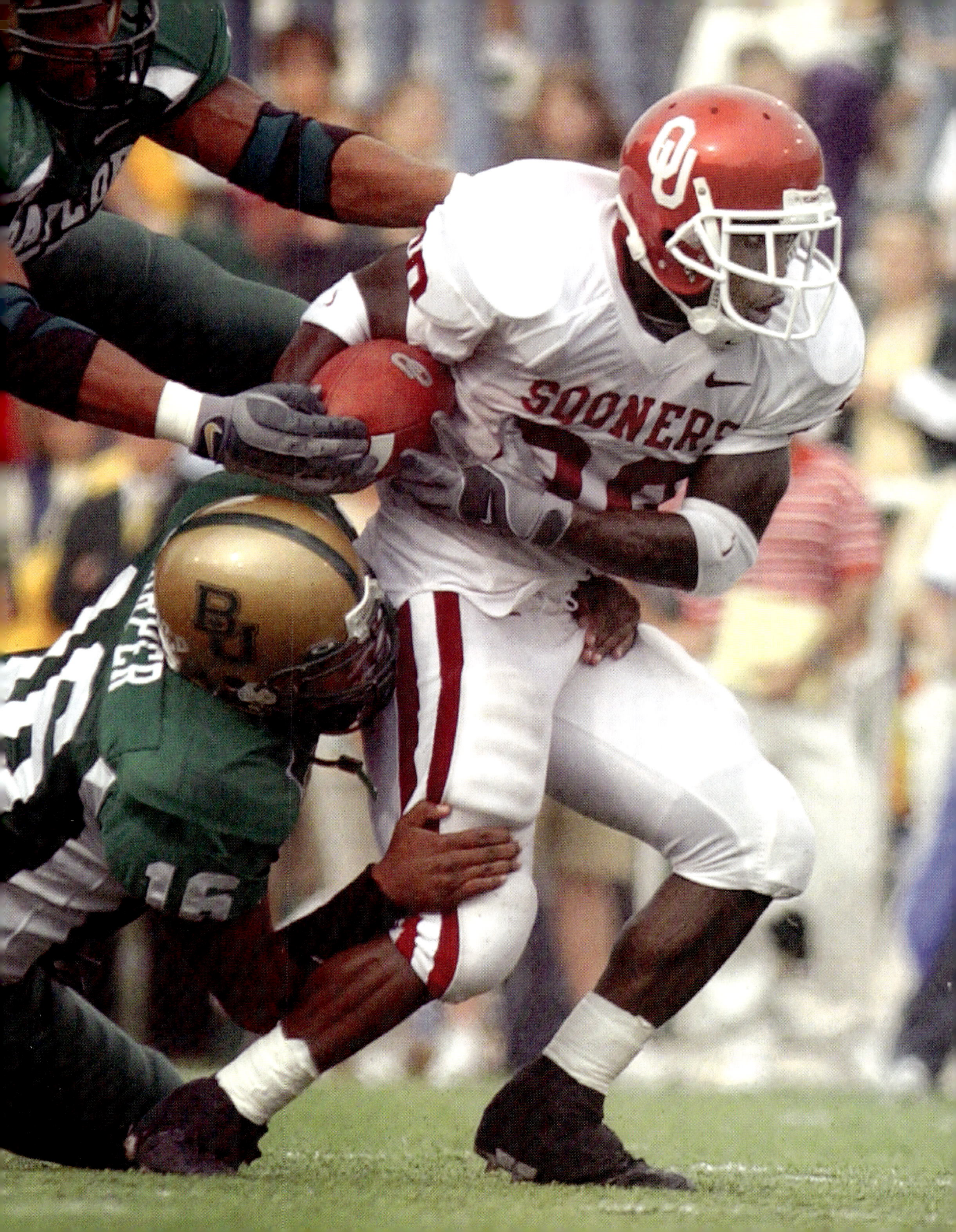
SOONERS
OU
BU
16

and found a rhythm — 9-of-12 for 80 yards, including plenty of short dump passes to reserve tailback Kejuan Jones.

When White hit Travis Wilson for a 10-yard touchdown with 21.2 seconds left in the half, OU led 14–0.

"That touchdown took the wind out of our sails," Baylor defensive back Maurice Linguist said.

And provided some momentum for the Sooners.

"Guys were kind of down, fussing at each other," Carter said. "It was important. We got a little momentum going into the second half."

Next hero: Adrian Peterson. A week after being held under 100 yards for the first time in his career, Peterson rolled for 240 and three touchdowns on 32 carries. He appeared fully healthy, with no lingering shoulder issues.

"The offensive line did a great job opening holes, and (fullback) J.D. (Runnels) and the receivers blocked well downfield," Peterson said. "There were a couple of plays where the line opened up big holes, and I just got tripped up."

Not too often, though. At least, not in the second half.

On the first play of the third quarter, Peterson romped for 49 yards. He scored a touchdown four plays later. And on OU's next possession, another touchdown drive, he carried six times for 64 yards.

"He rumbled today," senior receiver Brandon Jones said. "He had fresh legs. He ran really well."

Peterson's three touchdowns were a career-high, and he rushed for 100 yards for the 10th time, tying the NCAA record (also held by Wisconsin's Anthony Davis) for most 100-yard games by a freshman.

Once again, the opponents were impressed by Peterson.

"We knew he was pretty good," Baylor coach Guy Morriss said. "For a while, we were hitting him pretty good, and he got up a couple of times dizzy and limping. But he kept coming back on the field. He's a tough kid."

When OU scored again on its third possession of the third quarter – this one an impressive, 17-play, 93-yard drive that consumed 7:23 – the lead was 35–0.

Plenty of time for more points, right? Well, only if the reserves got it done.

OU finished with 302 rushing yards, 501 total. And White, who threw 25 passes in the first half, tossed just seven in the second half.

"We went out in the first half and tried to take a bunch of (passing) shots on 'em," said OU offensive tackle Wes Sims. "Then we went back to our game plan, just trying to wear 'em down."

Meanwhile, the OU defense notched its second shutout of the season – Texas was the other. Baylor managed just 156 total yards. The Sooners sacked quarterback Terrance Parks seven times.

Adrian Peterson broke free for 240 yards and three TDs against Baylor.

Photography by Laizure Photo

"Oklahoma, in my opinion, has the best defense in the Big 12. And it showed today," Parks said.

"Whenever you can hit the quarterback, it's fun," said OU end Jonathan Jackson, who recorded two sacks.

OU's ends, by the way, did most of the damage to Parks. Larry Birdine tied an OU single-game record with three sacks. Dan Cody added another.

"They smashed us," Baylor center Joe DeWoody said.

A word on the defense. Yeah, Baylor is Baylor, the Big 12 South's perennial cellar dweller. The Bears finished 3–8. But they had beaten Texas A&M in overtime.

And not so long earlier, OU's defense had been questioned after Oklahoma State and Texas A&M rolled up big numbers, mostly via the air. But in wins over Nebraska and Baylor, the Sooners allowed just three points.

"We came and played the way we wanted to," said co-defensive coordinator Brent Venables of the Sooners' effort against Baylor.

"We played sound," co-defensive coordinator Bo Pelini said. "We played with a sense of urgency for four quarters."

Another interesting development involved another true freshman. For the second time in three weeks, Stoops pulled the redshirt off a freshman. Against Texas A&M, it was cornerback Marcus Walker. Against Baylor, kicker Garrett Hartley replaced DiCarlo.

Here was the funny thing: Walker had told Hartley he wouldn't mind losing his redshirt, even so late in the season.

"Coming out of redshirt, he told me, was a cool feeling," Walker said. "He wasn't lying."

Hartley wasn't called on to kick a field goal, but he converted four extra points.

"It's pretty obvious," Stoops said. "Trey has just struggled. It got to the point, points matter too much, when you're looking at championship games in front of you."

Another development made with an eye on the future: Antonio Perkins, who hadn't returned punts since injuring a knee against Texas, returned to the role after Mark Clayton muffed a punt.

"It was a big step for him," Venables said. "Happy for him. When Mark made the mistake he did, you like to know you have those options, so you put the All-American out there."

And the Sooners put out another superlative effort.

"Anybody that watched the game could see that we dominated from start to finish," Birdine said. "You can only hope that it's good enough."

stats

Score by Quarters	1	2	3	4	Score	
Oklahoma	7	7	14	7	35	Record: (11-0,8-0)
Baylor	0	0	0	0	0	Record: (3-8,1-7)

Scoring Summary:
1st 10:33 OU - Clayton, Mark 19 yd pass from White, Jason (DiCarlo, Trey kick), 3-17 0:53, OU 7 - BU 0
2nd 00:21 OU - Wilson, Travis 10 yd pass from White, Jason (Hartley, Garret kick), 14-87 2:25, OU 14 - BU 0
3rd 12:57 OU - Peterson, Adrian 1 yd run (Hartley, Garret kick), 5-80 2:03, OU 21 - BU 0
  07:34 OU - Peterson, Adrian 1 yd run (Hartley, Garret kick), 8-74 3:38, OU 28 - BU 0
4th 11:29 OU - Peterson, Adrian 2 yd run (Hartley, Garret kick), 17-93 7:23, OU 35 - BU 0

	OU	BU
FIRST DOWNS	29	11
RUSHES-YARDS (NET)	47-302	31-26
PASSING YDS (NET)	199	130
Passes Att-Comp-Int	34-21-0	22-14-0
TOTAL OFFENSE PLAYS-YARDS	81-501	53-156
Fumble Returns-Yards	0-0	0-0
Punt Returns-Yards	2—3	3-14
Kickoff Returns-Yards	0-0	2-27
Interception Returns-Yards	0-0	0-0
Punts (Number-Avg)	4-40.5	7-47.3
Fumbles-Lost	0-0	1-1
Penalties-Yards	2-10	1-15
Possession Time	32:50	27:10
Third-Down Conversions	8 of 15	4 of 12
Fourth-Down Conversions	2 of 2	0 of 0
Red-Zone Scores-Chances	5-5	0-1
Sacks By: Number-Yards	7-52	0-0

RUSHING: Oklahoma-Peterson, Adrian 32-240; Jones, Kejuan 7-30; Choice, Tashard 6-29; Wolfe, D.J. 1-2; White, Jason 1-1. Baylor-Mosley, Paul 15-57; Golden, Jonathan 5-8; Team 1-0; Parks, Terrance 10-minus 39.

PASSING: Oklahoma-White, Jason 19-32-0-194; Grady, Tommy 2-2-0-5. Baylor-Parks, Terrance 14-22-0-130.

RECEIVING: Oklahoma-Jones, Kejuan 5-46; Moses, James 3-40; Clayton, Mark 3-35; Wilson, Travis 3-23; Finley, Joe Jon 2-21; Runnels, J.D. 2-19; Jones, Brandon 1-10; Choice, Tashard 1-7; Wolfe, D.J. 1-minus 2.
Baylor-Roberts, Marque 5-80; Evans, Jonathan 2-19; Rochon, Shaun 2-12; Fields, J 1-7; Venus, Marcus 1-7; Miller, Mike 1-3; Shelton, Trent 1-3; Golden, Jonathan 1-minus 1.

INTERCEPTIONS: Oklahoma-None. Baylor-None.

FUMBLES: Oklahoma-None. Baylor-Golden, Jonathan 1-1.

The Postseason

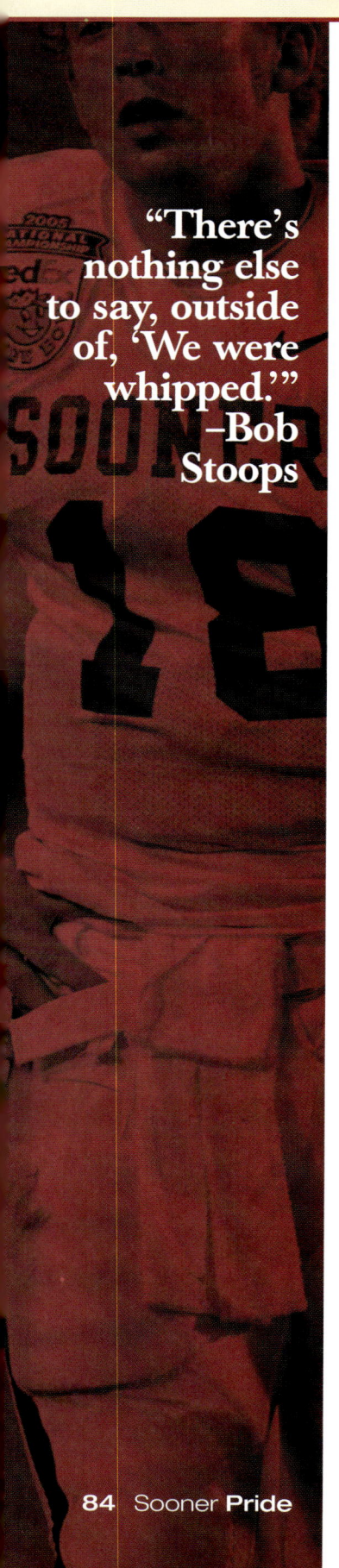

"There's nothing else to say, outside of, 'We were whipped.'"
—Bob Stoops

Orange Crush
USC 55, Oklahoma 19

Jan. 4, 2005

MIAMI, FL. - After it was over, after the long walk off the field, Mark Clayton shook his head. Never, in his wildest imagination, could he have envisioned this.

Southern California 55. Oklahoma 19.

"This is a tough cookie to eat," Oklahoma's senior receiver said. "This is pretty bad. … I can't explain it."

Are you kidding? The Orange Bowl matchup billed as one of the greatest in college football history was instead a mismatch of epic proportions. Top-ranked USC, a slight favorite over No. 2 OU, took advantage of four Sooner turnovers in the first half — turning them into 24 points — and the rout was on.

"It's not going to be an instant classic," USC tailback/receiver Reggie Bush said. "But it's a game that will go down in history."

It will go down better in some quarters than others.

USC won its second straight national championship — its first BCS title. And OU lost for the second straight time in a national championship game. It was the worst loss of the Bob Stoops era.

"There's nothing else to say, outside of, 'We were whipped,'" Stoops said.

The outcome was stunning. The Sooners (12-1) entered confident, riding a 12-game winning streak. They appeared to have exorcised the demons of 2003, when losses in the Big 12 championship and the Sugar Bowl turned a perfect season into a perfect nightmare, and to have corrected the flaws exposed during a midseason stretch of 2004.

Welcome back, demons. The Sooners' dreams of redemption were dashed by a talented band of Trojans. Though OU took an early 7–0 lead — Jason White led a 12-play, 92-yard drive — the wheels came off the Sooner Schooner soon afterward.

Four first-half turnovers deflated any chance OU had.

"That makes it pretty difficult to win," Stoops said.

The biggest was the first. Late in the first quarter, the game was tied at 7. OU's defense had stopped USC on two of its first three possessions. But when senior receiver Mark Bradley tried to field a bouncing punt — "a boneheaded mistake," he later said — the Trojans were handed a gift.

And the game, maybe.

The punt wasn't a great one. OU returner Antonio Perkins shied away from it as it skittered toward the end zone along the OU sideline. But at the last moment, Bradley grabbed the football; when he tried to race ahead, a defender poked it loose.

"I have no idea why Mark would have done that," Stoops said. "I was as shocked as everybody in the stadium. How do you explain that? I don't know. That goes back to Pop Warner football. Mark should have

USC bottled up the Sooners all night long.

Associated Press

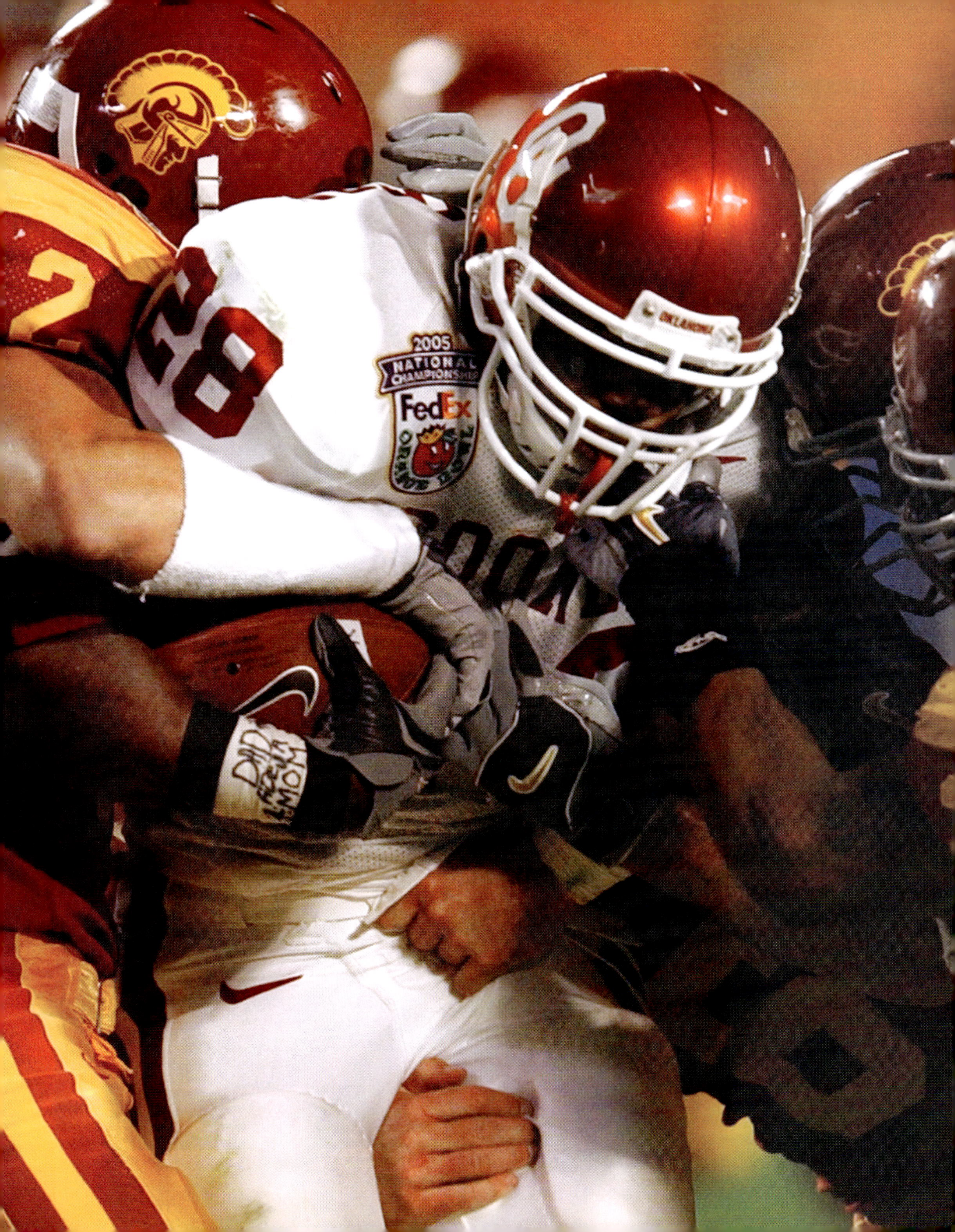
28
2005
NATIONAL CHAMPIONSHIP
FedEx

made a better decision."

USC recovered at the OU 6. LenDale White banged in for the go-ahead touchdown on the next play. And although USC's lead was only 14–7, the Sooners were deflated.

Next, White tossed his first interception, a jump ball toward Clayton – and three USC defensive backs. Safety Jason Leach came down with it. And USC quickly turned it into more points and a 21–7 lead.

"It was a horrible decision on my part," White said. "I should have just threw the ball away, and I didn't. I just tried to make a play."

Another possession resulted in another White interception. And again, USC turned it into a touchdown. Matt Leinart's 5-yard pass to Steve Smith pushed the Trojans up 28–7 with 9:17 left in the second quarter.

"You could see the frustration on their faces," USC linebacker Lofa Tutupu said. "You could hear a couple of guys yelling back and talking to each other. ... You start to see them break down."

And once USC got rolling, it wouldn't be stopped. Heisman Trophy winner Matt Leinart threw for 332 yards and an Orange Bowl-record five touchdowns, helping fuel an offense that produced 525 yards.

"It seemed like everything just fell apart," Clayton said. "Their surge was something we couldn't handle."

And USC's defense proved as formidable as expected. Though OU finished with 372 yards and 19 points, there were few highlights. A running game that averaged 215.1 yards during the first 12 games mustered 128. Adrian Peterson was held below 100 yards for the second time in a 13-game career.

And though White threw for 244 yards, he tossed three interceptions, including two in the first half, when the Trojans put the game away.

"It wasn't easy, but we made it look that way," said USC tight end Dominique Byrd, whose 33-yard touchdown reception was the Trojans' first score. "I think this was as close to perfect as you can get in this kind of setting, high pressure."

"The game went our way from the beginning," USC coach Pete Carroll said. "I was a little surprised, but we controlled all phases of the game tonight. ... We could have played all night long and kept having fun."

The Sooners had a slightly different experience.

"Disappointed, embarrassed, you name it," said White. "You make it all the way to the end, to what you really want, and you don't get it. And you know you left everything you had out there. I'm just disappointed and embarrassed.

"I think the whole team would say the same thing."

It was 38–10 at halftime. And the score would grow to 55–10 before the fourth quarter, when OU got a safety, then a touchdown to set the final margin. The cosmetic scores weren't nearly enough to cover the blemishes.

A few notables: The margin of defeat was

(above) Southern Cal's LenDale White (21) scores a touchdown despite Oklahoma's defensive effort during the second half. (right) Oklahoma's Travis Wilson (4) makes a touchdown catch as Southern Cal's Justin Wyatt (24) and Darnell Bing (20) defend.

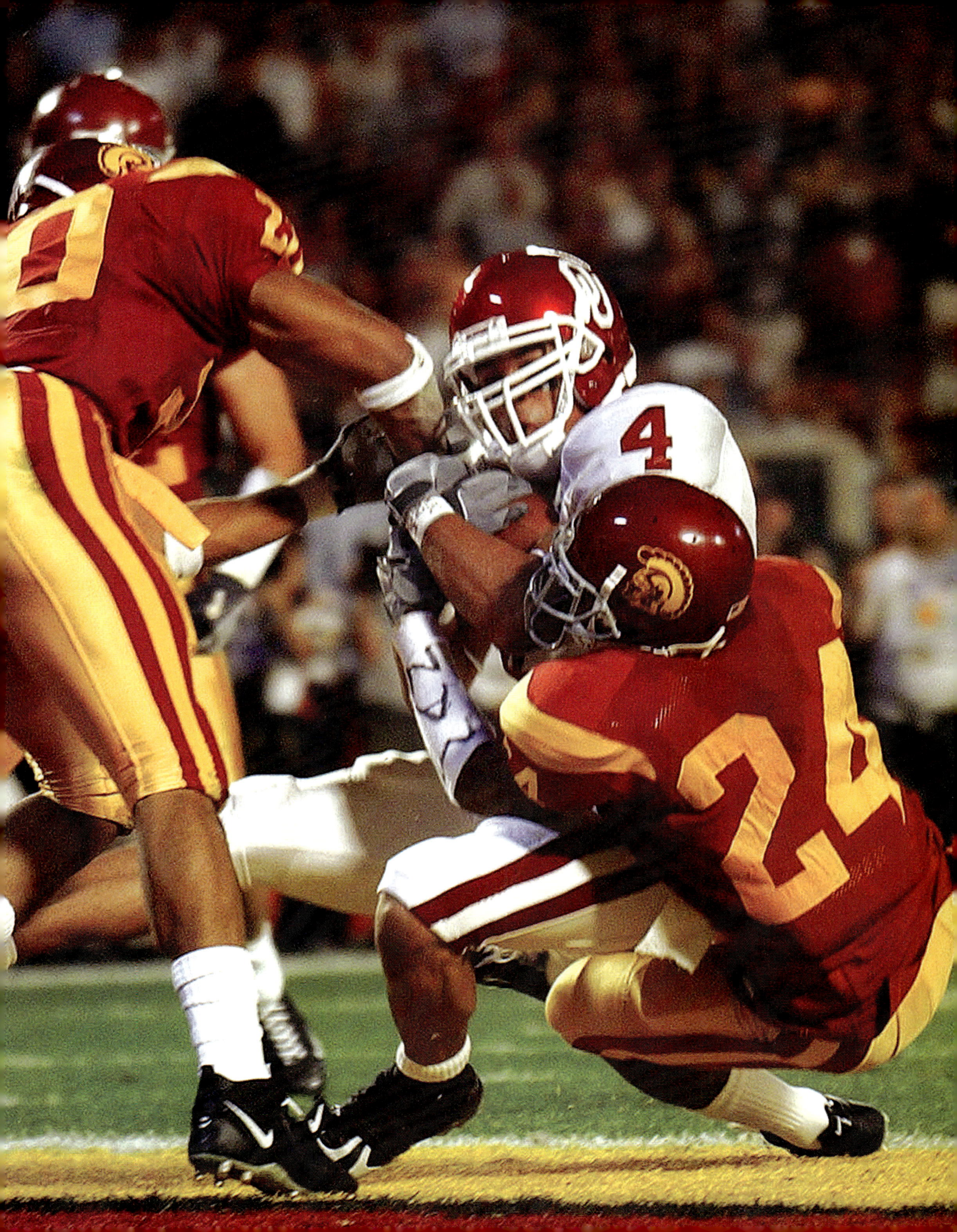

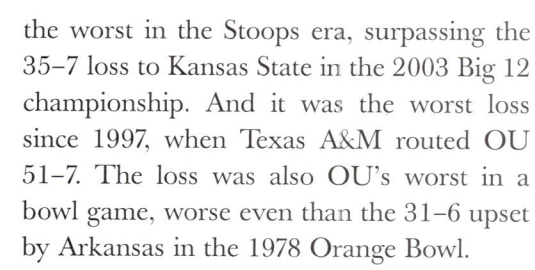

the worst in the Stoops era, surpassing the 35–7 loss to Kansas State in the 2003 Big 12 championship. And it was the worst loss since 1997, when Texas A&M routed OU 51–7. The loss was also OU's worst in a bowl game, worse even than the 31–6 upset by Arkansas in the 1978 Orange Bowl.

Afterward, the Sooners dutifully gave credit to USC. And rightfully so. But the Sooners couldn't help but think they hadn't given their best effort.

"I think they're great, but I don't know if that's a surprise to anybody," Stoops said. "We felt that way a week ago, and they proved it today. I think they're an excellent team. They play great as a team.

"You look at them today. They have no turnovers, just really executed in a great way, and they made the plays that counted. … They made the plays where it really mattered."

And OU? The team that had made "FINISH" its mantra didn't finish well at all. OU had committed just 13 turnovers in 12 games, but had five against USC.

"We turned the ball over, and that killed us in the first half," White said. "We were playing catch-up the rest of the time. You've got to give them credit. They played a great game, very well-coached, have great athletes and they made plays on both sides of the ball tonight.

"They came out to play. We didn't."

In the postgame locker room, Stoops told the Sooners to "learn from it, guys, that we're coming back."

"You can't get into these big games and make mistakes like we did," Stoops said. "You know, the turnovers early in a big game like this, you can't have them. And also, you can't give up big plays. In the end, that was it. That was the biggest part of it."

The game had been billed as determining college football's program of the decade. OU, after all, had won the 2000 national championship and was playing in its third title game in five years. And USC was playing for its second straight national championship.

"It's just crazy," Byrd said. "It puts us up there with the Miami Hurricanes, Nebraska and teams like that. It's just crazy to go

Oklahoma's J.D. Runnels (38) and quarterback Jason White react on the sideline during their 55–19 loss to Southern Cal.

Associated Press

down in history as back-to-back national champions."

Where the Sooners would go from there was uncertain. But Stoops was optimistic when asked how the Sooners would rebound from their second straight title-game loss.

"Hopefully, we can get in it again next year and have a shot to win," he said. "That's what happened a year ago and there weren't any far-reaching effects."

Still, OU must rebuild — or at least, reload. Twelve senior starters played their last game against USC. Among those departing: Jason White, Mark Clayton, Jammal Brown and Antonio Perkins. Stoops congratulated his team for its accomplishments in 2004, "for fighting through a tough year getting to this point."

"I don't take that for granted as a coach," Stoops said. "I appreciate their efforts. I'm not sitting here boasting or proud of what we did today, but it's a long year. They've worked hard. We didn't get it done tonight."

White, who came back for a sixth season in large part to win the Big 12 and national championships that eluded him in 2003, would have to settle for achieving one-half of his goals. The 2003 Heisman Trophy winner led OU to the conference title in 2004. But his career ended in empty fashion.

"It's a roller coaster," White said. "Sometimes you're high, sometimes you're low. Right now, it's at a low point. There's nothing I can do to go back and change it. It's not like I can come back next year and make up for it. It's at a low point, but I'll be all right.

"I just have to fight through, and the sun will come up tomorrow."

After the final seconds had ticked off the clock, most Sooners quickly vacated the premises, headed for the locker room. But senior cornerback Antonio Perkins, who had just finished playing his final game, lingered on the field, watching the Trojans' celebration.

"I just wanted to see what it is like to win a national championship," Perkins said. "I feel like I am playing for a program that should be winning national championships." ■

stats

Score by Quarters	1	2	3	4	Score
Oklahoma	7	3	0	9	19
USC	14	24	10	7	55

Scoring Summary:

1st 7:44 OU–Wilson, Travis 5 yd pass from White, Jason (Hartley, Garret kick), 12-92, 5:56, OU 7 – USC 0 4:27 USC–Byrd, Dominique 33 pass from Leinart, Matt (Killeen, Ryan kick), 6-75 yards, 3:17, OU 7 – USC 7 0:17 USC–White, LenDale 6 yd run (Killeen, Ryan kick), 1-6, 0:06, OU 7 – USC 14

2nd 11:46 USC–Jarrett, Dwayne 54 yd pass from Leinart, Matt (Killeen, Ryan kick), 6-89, 1:41, OU 7 – USC 21 9:17 USC–Smith, Steve 5 yd pass from Leinart, Matt (Killeen, Ryan kick), 3-10, 0:49, OU 7 – USC 28 3:10 OU–FG Hartley, Garret 29 yd, 13-68, 6:07, OU 10 – USC 28 1:56 USC–Smith, Steve, 33 yd pass from Leinart, Matt (Killeen, Ryan kick), 4-79, 1:14, OU 10 – USC 35 0:03 USC–FG Killeen, Ryan 44 yd, 7-8, 0:50, OU 10 – USC 38

3rd 10:42 USC–Smith, Steve 4 yd pass from Leinart, Matt (Killeen, Ryan kick), 8-85, 3:07, OU 10 – USC 45 4:01 USC–FG Killeen, Ryan 42 yd, 9-45, 2:34, OU 10 – USC 48

4th 9:46 USC–White, LenDale 8 yd run (Killeen, Ryan kick), 5-56, 3:00, OU 10 – USC 55
6:34 OU–Safety, Leinart, Matt downed in end zone, OU 12 – USC 55
3:59 OU–Wilson, Travis 9 pass from White, Jason (Hartley, Garret kick), 6-49, 2:35, OU 19 – USC 55

	OU	SC
FIRST DOWNS	19	19
RUSHES-YARDS (NET)	40-128	28-193
PASSING YDS (NET)	244	332
Passes Att-Comp-Int	36-24-3	35-18-0
TOTAL OFFENSIVE PLAYS-YARDS	76 -372	63-525
Punts Returns-Yards	1-3	1-7
Kickoffs Returns-Yards	7-139	2-36
Interceptions Returns-Yards	0-0	3-31
Punts (Number-Avg)	4-44.5	4-43.5
Fumbles-Lost	3-2	1-0
Penalties-Yards	3-30	9-75
Possession Time	35:06	24:54
Third-Down Conversions	8-17	6-14
Fourth-Down Conversions	0-1	2-2
Sacks by: Number-Yards	1-9	2-20

RUSHING: Oklahoma–Peterson, Adrian 25-82; Wolfe, D.J. 7-40; Jones, Kejuan 4-9; Wilson, Travis 1-5; White, Jason 3-(minus 8). USC–White, LenDale 15-118; Bush, Reggie 6-75; Kirtman, David 1-4; Webb, Lee 1-4; Reed, Desmond 2-2; Byrd, Dominique 1-1; Leinart, Matt 2-(minus 11).

PASSING: Oklahoma-White, Jason 24-36-3-244. USC-Leinart 18-35-0-332.

RECEIVING: Oklahoma–Wilson, Travis 7-59; Clayton, Mark 4-21; Bradley, Mark 2-66; Jones, Kejuan 2-30; Jones, Brandon 2-13; Peterson, Adrian 2-6; Rankins, Jejuan 2-0; Finley, Joe John 1-23; Peoples, Will 1-18; Moses, James 1-8. USC–Smith, Steve 7-113; Jarrett, Dwayne 5-115; Byrd, Dominique 3-58; Bush, Reggie 2-31; Kirtman, David 1-15.

INTERCEPTIONS: Oklahoma–None. USC–Wright, Eric 1-22; Grootegoed, Matt 1-9; Leach, Jason 1-0.

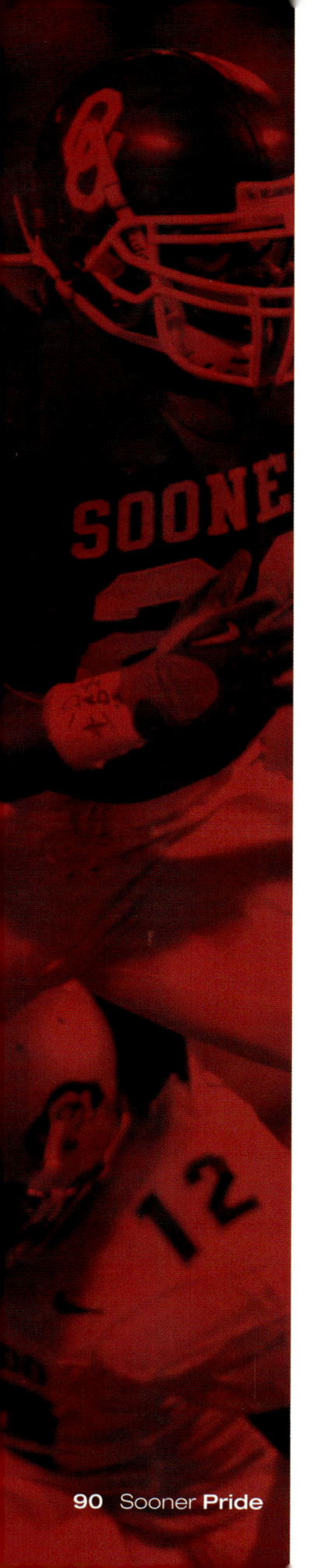

Oklahoma Football Tradition

If what distinguishes college football from every other sport in the world is its wealth of tradition, the University of Oklahoma is one of the game's great benefactors. Since the midpoint of the 20th century, Oklahoma has won more games and national titles than any other school.

The university was playing football 12 years before the state was admitted to the union. In 1895, the same year crimson and cream were adopted as the official school colors, OU played its first football game.

Contrary to most casual fans' perception, the legendary Bud Wilkinson was not the coach who put Oklahoma football on the map. Bennie Owen had compiled a record of 122–54–16 and fielded four undefeated teams as Sooner head man from 1905-1926. Owen is a charter member of the College Football Hall of Fame, and the playing field in OU's Memorial Stadium is named for him.

But it was after World War II that the Sooners rose to national supremacy. Wilkinson had been an All-America guard on Bernie Bierman's great Minnesota teams of the mid-1930s. He learned the split-T attack from its inventor, Don Faurot, while he and Jim Tatum were assistants under Faurot at Iowa Preflight during World War II. Tatum served as OU's head coach in 1946, and after one year bolted for Maryland. Wilkinson was promoted from assistant to head coach in 1947, and the rest is college football history.

Wilkinson posted a record of 145–29–4 with three national titles as Sooner mentor from 1947-1963. His .826 winning percentage ranks ninth all-time among Division I-A coaches. Wilkinson's teams once strung together 47 straight victories, an apparently unassailable NCAA record, from 1953-1957. The streak included three straight perfect seasons and consecutive national titles in 1955 and '56. Lost behind the glare of a 47-game winning streak is the fact that Wilkinson also coached the Sooners to 31 straight victories from 1948-1950, culminating in the 1950 national title.

From 1948 through 1959, Oklahoma won 12 straight conference championships, including all 10 Big Seven titles and the first two in the Big Eight after Oklahoma State came aboard in 1958. In 1952, Sooner halfback Billy Vessels won the Heisman Trophy.

Wilkinson's masterpiece was the 1956 unit, a juggernaut that's always mentioned when the topic turns to the greatest football teams of all time. Two of the All-Americans from that unforgettable team — halfback Tommy McDonald and center/linebacker Jerry Tubbs — are

Billy Sims

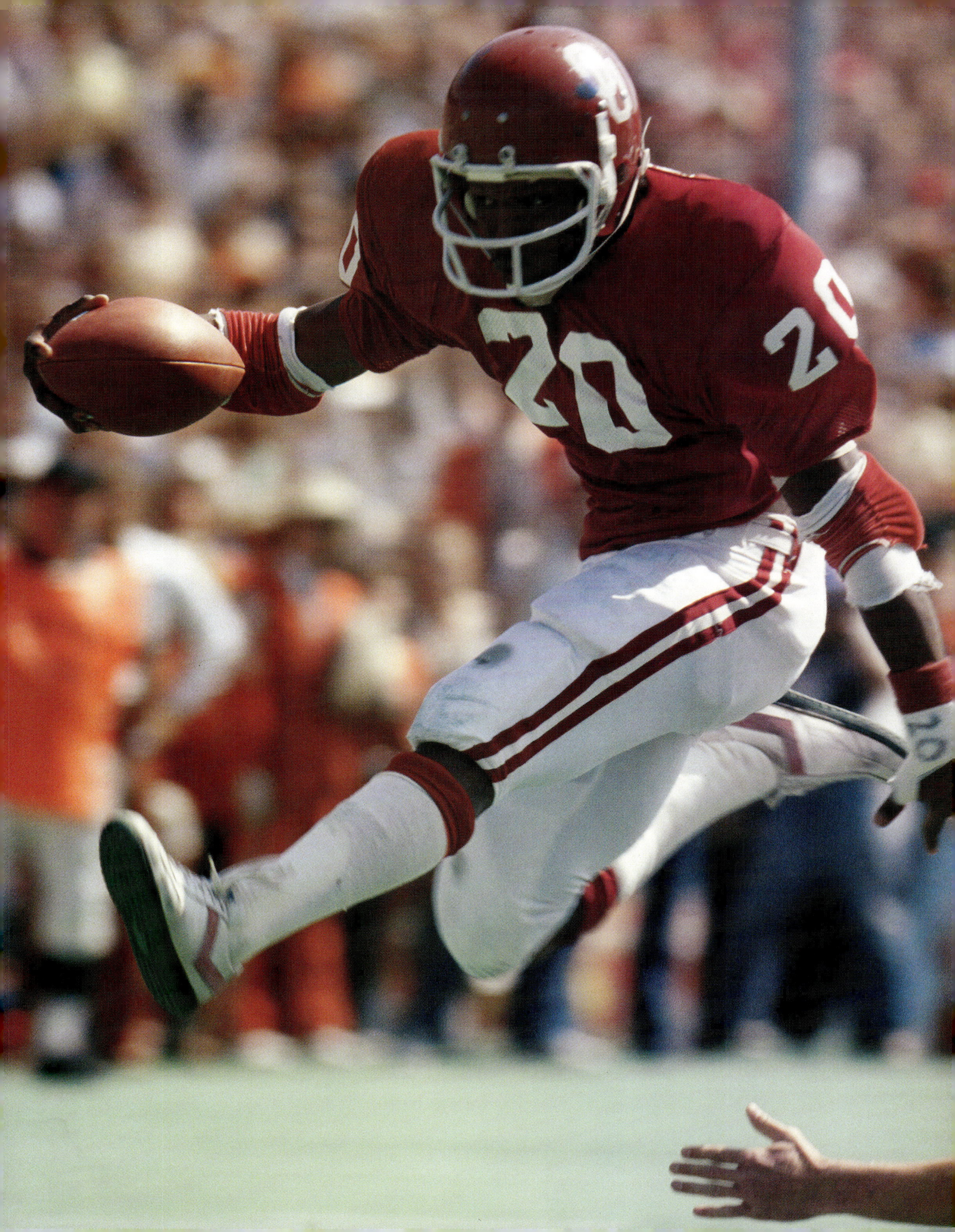
20

92 Sooner Pride

Sooner **Pride** 93

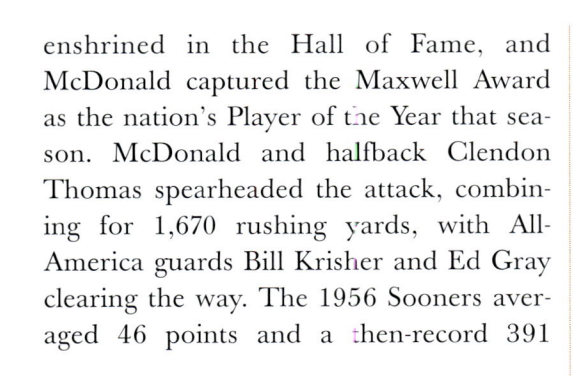

enshrined in the Hall of Fame, and McDonald captured the Maxwell Award as the nation's Player of the Year that season. McDonald and halfback Clendon Thomas spearheaded the attack, combining for 1,670 rushing yards, with All-America guards Bill Krisher and Ed Gray clearing the way. The 1956 Sooners averaged 46 points and a then-record 391 rushing yards, shut out six opponents and were never challenged. They began the campaign by whitewashing North Carolina 36-0, Kansas State 66-0 and Texas 45-0, and closed with wins of 54-6 over Nebraska and 53-0 over Oklahoma State. At midseason came a 40-0 victory at Notre Dame. The Sooners finished the year with 40 straight wins and kept on winning until late in the following season.

Wilkinson's departure after an 8-2 campaign in 1963 didn't take OU out of the national championship business. Indeed, the Sooners were just getting started. Barry Switzer stood at the helm in Norman for 16 years in the 1970s and 80s and posted a record of 157-29-4. Switzer's career winning percentage of .837 ranks fourth-best all-time on the D-IA charts — even higher than Wilkinson's — and his teams added three more national titles (1974, 1975, 1985) to the OU legend.

Switzer came to Norman as offensive line coach in 1966 and was promoted to offensive coordinator in 1967. In 1970, he talked then-head coach Chuck Fairbanks into installing a wishbone offense, and a second Oklahoma dynasty was born. Tailback Steve Owens had just put the finishing touches on his magnificent career and brought the Heisman Trophy to Norman in 1969. To this day, no Sooner has ever scored touchdowns with greater frequency than Owens did. No.

The legendary Bud Wilkinson led Sooner winning streaks of 47 and 31 games.

94 Sooner **Pride**

36 hit paydirt 56 times, and he did it all in the space of a three-year career.

Jack Mildren took over at quarterback as a sophomore in Owens' Heisman year of 1969 and directed the Oklahoma wishbone through its maiden voyage the following season. Mildren was an All-American in 1971, when he set a still-standing school record with a 209.9 passing efficiency rating. Two-year All-America halfback Greg Pruitt ignited the OU running game in 1971 and 72, finishing as Heisman Trophy runner-up as a senior.

Switzer ascended to head coach in 1973 and did not lose a game until 1975. Halfback Joe Washington spearheaded the Sooner attack for the first three years of Switzer's reign. Washington was another two-year All-American and third-place vote-getter in the 1974 Heisman race.

Helping ease Switzer into his role was the presence of not one, not two, but three Selmons – Lucious, Lee Roy and Dewey – on the defensive line. All three were starters in that 1973 campaign. During the Wilkinson years, Jim Weatherall and J.D. Roberts had won Outland Trophies as the nation's outstanding linemen in 1951 and 1953. Under Switzer, Lee Roy Selmon and offensive guard Greg Roberts added their names to the Outland roll call in 1975 and '78, respectively.

Defensive lineman Tony Casillas and tight end Keith Jackson were two-year consensus All-Americans, and Rickey Dixon took home a Thorpe Award as the nation's best defensive back in 1987. As for wishbone quarterbacks, four-year starter Jamelle Holieway is arguably the best who ever played. Holieway guided the Sooners to their sixth national title as a true freshman in 1985.

Also on Switzer's watch came two of the most decorated football players ever to don the crimson and cream – halfback Billy Sims, winner of both the Heisman and Walter Camp Trophies in 1978, and two-time Butkus Award-winning linebacker Brian Bosworth in the mid-'80s.

And now yet another Oklahoma dynasty rules college football. Bob Stoops became head coach in 1999, and his program seized the throne the very next season after rampaging through a 13–0 no-doubter. Over Stoops' first two years, quarterback Josh Heupel set a new standard for Oklahoma passers, surpassing the single-season marks Cale Gundy had established less than a decade earlier.

The final jewel in OU's 2000 national crown came in the form of a 13–2 Orange Bowl victory over Florida State, a contest in which the Sooner defense accomplished the unimaginable by blanking the Seminole offense. Heupel had finished second to Florida State quarterback Chris Weinke in the Heisman voting but came away with the biggest prize of all that night.

Quarterbacks Heupel and Jason White, linebackers Rocky Calmus and Teddy Lehman, cornerback Derrick Strait, safety Roy Williams and defensive tackle Tommie Harris lead the cavalcade of stars from the Stoops era into Sooner lore. And after his 1,884-yard campaign in 2002, Quentin Griffin climbed to fourth place on one of the most prestigious lists in all of football: Oklahoma's career rushing leaders.

The 1956 Sooners were famous for routing opponents, but the 2003 team outdid even that legendary team. The 03 Sooners were the highest-scoring team in the land, surpassing the 50-point mark in seven different regular-season games. The margin of victory in OU's 77–0 rout of Texas A&M set a new Big 12 record, and Stoops' offense had to find creative ways to keep the score down.

If the Sooner Schooner were weighted down with all of Oklahoma's national championship trophies and individual awards, Boomer and Sooner would be one pooped-out pair of ponies. No one has been ranked No. 1 in the Associated Press poll more often than the Sooners, and OU's assault on the rankings will continue as long as Bob Stoops runs the show.

And as satisfying as the Sooners' dominance has been, the 2004 season may be as gratifying as any that OU fans have experienced in their century of gridiron excellence. A cloud of disappointment hung in the Norman air following last season's mini-collapse, but this year's edition has played with uncommon focus and determination, against longer odds, en route to the Sooners' eighth national championship.

It's great to be a Sooner. And it's only getting better. ∎

Sooner Spirit

From the famed Sooner Schooner to the Red River Shootout, from Bennie Owen to Bud Wilkinson to Barry Switzer, the tradition that is Oklahoma football has entertained and captivated Sooner fans for over 100 years.

98 Sooner **Pride**

Sooner **Pride** 99

100 Sooner **Pride**

Sooner **Pride** 101

102 Sooner Pride

Sooner Pride 103

104 Sooner Pride

Sooner Pride 105

Statistics

Team Stats	OU	OPP
SCORING	433	164
Points Per Game	36.1	13.7
FIRST DOWNS	291	184
Rushing	138	67
Passing	135	99
Penalty	18	18
RUSHING YARDAGE	2581	1037
Yards gained rushing	2842	1428
Yards lost rushing	261	391
Rushing Attempts	525	374
Average Per Rush	4.9	2.8
Average Per Game	215.1	86.4
TDs Rushing	22	8
PASSING YARDAGE	3054	2325
Att-Comp-Int	370-244-6	375-205-8
Average Per Pass	8.3	6.2
Average Per Catch	12.5	11.3
Average Per Game	254.5	193.8
TDs Passing	34	10
TOTAL OFFENSE	5635	3362
Total Plays	895	749
Average Per Play	6.3	4.5
Average Per Game	469.6	280.2
KICK RETURNS: #-YARDS	21-395	33-517
PUNT RETURNS: #-YARDS	34-313	21-88
INT RETURNS: #-YARDS	8-120	6-121
KICK RETURN AVERAGE	18.8	15.7
PUNT RETURN AVERAGE	9.2	4.2
INT RETURN AVERAGE	15.0	20.2
FUMBLES-LOST	17-7	17-14
PENALTIES-YARDS	82-703	74-577
Average Per Game	58.6	48.1
PUNTS-YARDS	49-2006	80-3319
Average Per Punt	40.9	41.5
Net punt average	39.1	37.6
TIME OF POSSESSION/GAME	33:02	26:58
3RD-DOWN CONVERSIONS	100/183	60/168
3rd-Down Pct	55%	36%
4TH-DOWN CONVERSIONS	12/16	6/15
4th-Down Pct	75%	40%
SACKS BY-YARDS	38-249	7-53
MISC YARDS	28	8
TOUCHDOWNS SCORED	59	21
FIELD GOALS-ATTEMPTS	8-16	6-9
PAT-ATTEMPTS	55-58	20-21
ATTENDANCE	507189	214454
Games/Avg Per Game	6/84532	4/53614
Neutral Site Games		2/70858

Score by Quarter	1st	2nd	3rd	4th	Total
Oklahoma Sooners	80	158	121	74	433
Opponents	35	51	34	44	164

RUSHING	GP	Att	Gain	Loss	Net	Avg	TD	Long	Avg/G
Peterson, Adrian	12	314	1955	112	1843	5.9	15	80	153.6
Jones, Kejuan	11	125	522	18	504	4.0	5	26	45.8
Choice, Tashard	8	22	100	0	100	4.5	0	14	12.5
Bradley, Mark	12	4	73	0	73	18.2	1	51	6.1
Wolfe, D.J.	12	18	69	2	67	3.7	0	31	5.6
Hickson, Donta	5	10	61	9	52	5.2	1	25	10.4
Clayton, Mark	12	4	19	8	11	2.8	0	16	0.9
Grady, Tommy	4	1	9	0	9	9.0	0	9	2.2
TEAM	5	7	0	30	-30	-4.3	0	0	-6.0
White, Jason	12	20	34	82	-48	-2.4	0	6	-4.0
Total	12	525	2842	261	2581	4.9	22	80	215.1
Opponents	12	374	1428	391	037	2.8	8	48	86.4

PASSING	GP	Effic	Att-Cmp-Int	Pct	Yds	TD	Lng	Avg/G
White, Jason	12	162.89	354-231-6	65.3	2961	33	72	246.8
Grady, Tommy	4	147.09	14-12-0	85.7	63	1	10	15.8
TEAM	5	0.00	1-0-0	0.0	0	0	0	0.0
Bradley, Mark	12	352.00	1-1-0	100.0	30	0	30	2.5
Total	12	162.36	370-244-6	65.9	3054	34	72	254.5
Opponents	12	111.28	375-205-8	54.7	2325	10	78	193.8

RECEIVING	GP	No.	Yds	Avg	TD	Long	Avg/G
Clayton, Mark	12	62	855	13.8	8	61	71.2
Wilson, Travis	12	43	601	14.0	9	41	50.1
Jones, Brandon	12	25	332	13.3	3	69	27.7
Bradley, Mark	12	21	425	20.2	7	72	35.4
Jones, Kejuan	11	20	166	8.3	0	23	15.1
Peoples, Will	12	19	206	10.8	2	28	17.2
Moses, James	12	16	143	8.9	2	40	11.9
Runnels, J.D.	12	14	133	9.5	1	23	11.1
Finley, Joe Jon	11	6	71	11.8	1	24	6.5
Rankins, Jejuan	9	4	48	12.0	0	17	5.3
Wolfe, D.J.	12	3	29	9.7	0	27	2.4
Peterson, Adria	12	3	6	2.0	0	6	0.5
Ford, Ataleo	6	2	14	7.0	0	10	2.3
Hickson, Donta	5	2	-3	-1.5	0	0	-0.6
Roberts, Willie	12	1	13	13.0	1	13	1.1
Choice, Tashard	8	1	7	7.0	0	7	0.9
Robinson, David	1	1	5	5.0	0	5	5.0
Townsend, Dan	5	1	3	3.0	0	3	0.6
Total	12	244	3054	12.5	34	72	254.5
Opponents	12	205	2325	11.3	10	78	193.8

SCORING	TD	FGs	PATs	DXP	Saf	Points
Peterson, Adrian	15	0-0	0-0	0	0	90
DiCarlo, Trey	0	8-16	45-48	0	0	69
Clayton, Mark	9	0-0	0-0	0	0	54
Wilson, Travis	9	0-0	0-0	0	0	54
Bradley, Mark	8	0-0	0-0	0	0	48
Jones, Kejuan	5	0-0	0-0	0	0	30
Jones, Brandon	3	0-0	0-0	0	0	18
Moses, James	2	0-0	0-0	0	0	12
Peoples, Will	2	0-0	0-0	0	0	12
Hartley, Garret	0	0-0	10-10	0	0	10
Roberts, Willie	1	0-0	0-0	0	0	6
Hickson, Donta	1	0-0	0-0	0	0	6
Finley, Joe Jon	1	0-0	0-0	0	0	6
Runnels, J.D.	1	0-0	0-0	0	0	6
Perkins, Antonio	1	0-0	0-0	0	0	6
Mitchell, Lance	1	0-0	0-0	0	0	6
White, Jason	0	0-0	0-0	0	0	0
Total	59	8-16	55-58	0	0	433
Opponents	21	6-9	20-21	0	0	164S

The National Championships

1950 — 10–1
Coach: Bud Wilkinson
Captains: Harry Moore, Blackwell, OK; Norman McNabb, Norman, OK

Date	Opponent	Result	Score
S.30	Boston College	W	28–0
O.7	Texas A&M	W	34–28
O.14	Texas at Dallas	W	14–13
O.21	Kansas State	W	58–0
O.28	at Iowa State	W	20–7
N.4	at Colorado	W	27–18
N.11	at Kansas	W	33–13
N.18	Missouri	W	41–7
N.25	Nebraska	W	49–35
D.2	at Oklahoma State	W	41–14

Sugar Bowl

J.1	Kentucky	L	7–13

Statistical Leaders
Rushing: Billy Vessels, 870 yards, 15 TDs
Passing: Claud Arnold, 1,048 yards, 13 TDs
Receiving: Billy Vessels, 11 rec., 229 yards, 2 TDs

1955 — 11–0
Coach: Bud Wilkinson
Captains: Bo Bolinger, Muskogee, OK; Cecil Morris, Lawton, OK; Bob Loughridge, Poteau, OK

Date	Opponent	Result	Score
S.24	at North Carolina	W	13–6
O.1	Pittsburgh	W	26–14
O.8	Texas at Dallas	W	20–0
O.15	Kansas	W	44–6
O.22	Colorado	W	56–21
O.29	at Kansas State	W	40–7
N.5	at Missouri	W	20–0
N.12	Iowa State	W	52–0
N.19	at Nebraska	W	41–0
N.26	Oklahoma State	W	53–0

Orange Bowl

J.1	Maryland	W	20–6

Statistical Leaders
Rushing: Tommy McDonald, 702 yards, 14 TDs
Passing: Tommy McDonald, 265 yards, 0 TDs
Receiving: Joe Mobra, 6 rec., 128 yards, 1 TD

1956 — 10–0
Coach: Bud Wilkinson
Captains: Ed Gray, Odessa, TX; Jerry Tubbs, Breckenridge, TX

Date	Opponent	Result	Score
S.29	North Carolina	W	36–0
O.6	Kansas State	W	66–0
O.13	Texas at Dallas	W	45–0
O.20	at Kansas	W	34–12
O.27	at Notre Dame	W	40–0
N.3	at Colorado	W	27–19
N.10	at Iowa State	W	44–0
N.17	Missouri	W	67–14
N.24	Nebraska	W	54–6
D.1	at Oklahoma State	W	53–0

Statistical Leaders
Rushing: Tommy McDonald, 853 yards, 12 TDs
Passing: Jimmy Harris, 482 yards, 8 TDs
Receiving: Tommy McDonald, 12 rec. 282 yards, 4 TDs

1974 — 11–0
Coach: Barry Switzer
Captains: Steve Davis, Sallisaw, OK; Kyle Davis, Altus, OK; Rod Shoate, Spiro, OK; Randy Hughes, Tulsa, OK

Date	Opponent	Result	Score
S.14	Baylor	W	28–11
S.28	Utah State	W	72–3
O.5	Wake Forest	W	63–0
O.12	Texas at Dallas	W	16–13
O.19	at Colorado	W	49–14
O.26	Kansas State	W	63–0
N.2	at Iowa State	W	28–10
N.9	Missouri	W	37–0
N.16	at Kansas	W	45–14
N.23	at Nebraska	W	28–14
N.30	Oklahoma State	W	44–13

Statistical Leaders
Rushing: Joe Washington, 1,321 yards, 13 TDs
Passing: Steve Davis, 601 yards, 11 TDs
Receiving: Tinker Owens, 18 rec., 413 yards, 5 TDs

1975 — 11–1
Coach: Barry Switzer
Captains: Lee Roy Selmon, Eufala, OK; Dewey Selmon, Eufala, OK; Joe Washington, Port Arthur, TX; Steve Davis, Sallisaw, OK

Date	Opponent	Result	Score
S.13	Oregon	W	62–7
S.20	Pittsburgh	W	46–10
S.26	at Miami, Fla.	W	20–17
O.4	Colorado	W	21–20
O.11	Texas at Dallas	W	24–17
O.18	at Kansas State	W	25–3
O.25	Iowa State	W	39–7
N.1	at Oklahoma State	W	27–7
N.8	Kansas	L	3–23
N.15	at Missouri	W	28–27
N.22	Nebraska	W	35–10

Orange Bowl

J.1	Michigan	W	14–6

Statistical Leaders
Rushing: Joe Washington, 871 yards, 11 TDs
Passing: Steve Davis, 438 yards, 1 TD
Receiving: Tinker Owens, 9 rec., 241 yards, 1 TD

1985 — 11–1
Coach: Barry Switzer
Captains: Tony Casillas, Tulsa, OK; Kevin Murphy, Richardson, TX; Eric Pope, Seminole, OK

Date	Opponent	Result	Score
S.28	at Minnesota	W	13–7
O.5	at Kansas State	W	41–6
O.12	Texas at Dallas	W	14–7
O.19	Miami, Fla.	L	14–27
O.26	Iowa State	W	59–14
N.2	Kansas	W	48–6
N.9	at Missouri	W	51–6
N.16	Colorado	W	31–0
N.23	Nebraska	W	27–7
N.30	at Oklahoma State	W	13–0
D.7	SMU	W	35–13

Orange Bowl

J.1	Penn State	W	25–10

Statistical Leaders
Rushing: Jamelle Holieway, 861 yards, 8 TDs
Passing: Jamelle Holieway, 517 yards, 5 TDs
Receiving: Keith Jackson, 20 rec., 486 yards, 2 TDs

2000 — 13–0
Coach: Bob Stoops
Captains: Josh Heupel, Aberdeen, SD; Seth Littrell, Muskogee, OK; Chris Hammons, Sulphur, OK; Rocky Calmus, Jenks, OK; Torrance Marshall, Miami, FL; Bubba Burcham, Mustang, OK

Date	Opponent	Result	Score
S.2	UTEP	W	55–14
S.9	Arkansas State	W	45–7
S.23	Rice	W	42–14
S.30	Kansas	W	34–16
O.7	Texas at Dallas	W	53–14
O.14	at Kansas State	W	41–31
O.28	Nebraska	W	31–14
N.4	at Baylor	W	56–7
N.11	at Texas A&M	W	35–31
N.18	Texas Tech	W	27–13
N.25	at Oklahoma State	W	12–7
D.2	Kansas State	W	27–24

Orange Bowl

J.3	Florida State	W	13–2

Statistical Leaders
Rushing: Quenton Griffin, 696 yards, 16 TDs
Passing: Josh Heupel, 3,172 yards, 18 TDs
Receiving: Antwone Savage, 47 rec., 594 yards, 3 TDs

Roster

#	Name	Pos	Ht	Wt	Yr	Hometown (School)
42	Alexander, Rufus	LB	6'1"	225	So.	Baton Rouge, La. (Christian Life)
48	Allen, Gayron	LB	5'10"	235	Sr.	Orange, Texas (West Orange Stark HS)
93	Ayodele, Remi	DT	6'3"	301	Jr.	Grand Prairie, Texas (NE Oklahoma A&M)
16	Baker, Lewis	LB	6'3"	210	So.	Carrollton, Texas (Hebron HS)
13	Bassey, Eric	DB	6'1"	199	Jr.	Garland, Texas (North Garland HS)
97	Bennett, Cory	DE	6'3"	265	Fr.	Garland, Texas (Roosevelt HS)
92	Birdine, Larry	DE	6'4"	254	So.	Lawton, Okla. (Eisenhower HS)
7	Bomar, Rhett	QB	6'4"	208	Fr.	Grand Prairie, Texas (Grand Prairie HS)
27	Bothun, Garrett	WR	5'11"	185	So.	Rowlett, Texas
14	Bowers, Brett	S	6'1"	193	Fr.	Jacksonville, Fla. (Trinity Christian Academy)
1	Bradley, Mark	WR	6'2"	198	Sr.	Pine Bluff, Ark. (Arkansas-Pine Bluff)
55	Brown, Jammal	OL	6'6"	313	Sr.	Lawton, Okla. (MacArthur HS)
52	Bush, Chris	OL	6'4"	284	Jr.	Channelview, Texas (Channelview HS)
31	Cade, Tony	DB	6'2"	205	RFr.	Lewisville, Texas (Lewisville HS)
6	Carter, Jason	DB	6'0"	195	So.	Tulsa, Okla. (Jenks HS)
50	Carter, Vince	OL	6'3"	294	Sr.	Waco, Texas (Waco HS)
70	Chaisson, Kelvin	OL	6'5"	303	Jr.	Beaumont, Texas (Ozen HS)
15	Chambers, Wayne	LB	6'3"	240	Jr.	Grandview, Mo. (Grandview HS)
19	Chaney, Quentin	WR	6'6"	205	Fr.	Tulsa, Okla. (Booker T. Washington)
64	Chester, Chris	OL	6'4"	278	Jr.	Tustin, Calif. (Tustin HS)
2	Choice, Tashard	RB	6'1"	205	RFr.	Lovejoy, Ga. (Lovejoy HS)
9	Clayton, Mark	WR	5'11"	187	Sr	Arlington, Texas (Sam Houston HS)
80	Cody, Dan	DE	6'5"	270	Sr.	Ada, Okla. (Ada HS)
90	Coleman, Steven	DL	6'5"	286	RFr.	Dallas, Texas (Skyline HS)
74	Dampeer, Lawrence	DL	6'3"	300	RFr.	Decatur, Ill. (MacArthur HS)
86	Davis, Alan	DE	6'2"	245	Fr.	Colleyville, Texas (Heritage HS)
36	Dennison, Russell	LB	6'3"	236	Jr.	Weatherford, Okla. (Weatherford HS)
83	DiCarlo, Trey	K	6'0"	204	Jr.	Carrollton, Texas (Creekview HS)
30	Dixon, Dan	DB	6'0"	186	Jr.	Tulsa, Okla. (Cornell University)
91	Dotson, Alonzo	DE	6'4"	241	RFr.	Alief, Texas (Hastings HS)
87	Ferguson, Blake	P	6'0"	190	Sr.	Broken Arrow, Okla. (Univ. of North Carolina)
85	Finley, Joe Jon	TE	6'6"	23	RFr.	Arlington, Texas (Arlington HS)
73	Flynn, John	OL	6'1"	242	Sr.	Anadarko, Okla. (Anadarko HS)
26	Ford, Ataleo	WR	6'1"	189	Sr.	Ardmore, Okla. (Ardmore HS)
17	Freeby, Cody	P	6'3"	217	RFr.	Fort Worth, Texas (Fort Worth Christian HS)
72	Garibay, Randy	OL	6'2"	231	Sr.	Lawton, Okla. (MacArthur HS)
15	Grady, Tommy	QB	6'6"	219	RFr.	Huntington Beach, Calif (Edison HS)
45	Greene, Jordan	DE	6'3"	240	Jr.	Colleyville, Texas (Heritage H.S.)
21	Gutierrez, Jacob	RB	5'7"	181	RFr.	San Antonio, Texas (Madison HS)
67	Hallock, Michael	OL	6'2"	220	Jr.	Plano, Texas (Plano HS)
26	Harris, R.J.	DB	5'10"	186	RFr.	Arlington, Texas (Arlington HS)
32	Hartley, Garrett	K	5'9"	175	Fr.	Southlake, Texas (Southlake Carroll HS)
35	Hickson, Donta	RB	5'10"	203	Jr.	McKinney, Texas (McKinney HS)
11	Holmes, Lendy	WR	6'2"	180	Fr.	Dallas, Texas (South Oak Cliff HS)
95	Hulsey, Grant	DE	6'5"	245	Sr.	Tuttle, Okla. (Tuttle HS)
44	Ingram, Clint	LB	6'2"	241	Jr.	Hallsville, Texas (Hallsville HS)
49	Jackson, Jonathan	DE	6'3"	250	Sr.	Houston, Texas (North Shore HS)
81	Jones, Brandon	WR	6'3"	214	Sr.	Texarkana, Texas (Liberty Eylau HS)
20	Jones, Kejuan	RB	5'9"	200	Jr.	Tulsa, Okla. (Jenks HS)
77	Joseph, Davin	OL	6'4"	312	Jr.	Hallandale, Fla. (Hallandale HS)
46	Latimer, Zach	LB	6'3"	231	So.	Denver, Colo. (Gateway HS)
17	Lippe, Tyler	DB	6'0"	190	So.	Austin, Texas
27	Luna, Jacob	DB	5'11"	192	Jr.	Grapevine, Texas (Grapevine H.S.)
66	McAdams, Randy	OL	6'7"	285	Fr.	Leander, Texas (Leander HS)
96	McGruder, Lynn	DL	6'3"	302	Sr.	Las Vegas, Nev. (Univ. of Tennessee)
79	Messner, Chris	OL	6'7"	278	So.	Frederick, Okla. (Frederick HS)
69	Millington, Akim	OL	6'6"	300	RFr.	Wheaton, Ill. (Wheaton North HS)
10	Mitchell, Lance	LB	6'3"	244	Sr.	Los Banos, Calif. (City College of San Francisco)
89	Moses, James	TE	6'3"	246	Sr.	Houston, Texas (North Shore HS)
8	Nicholson, Donte	DB	6'2"	216	Sr.	Ramona, Calif. (Mt. San Antonio JC)
82	Nixon, Laenar	DE	6'3"	228	So.	Miami, Fla. (Carol City HS)
22	Onyenegecha, Chijioke	DB	6'2"	205	Jr.	Richmond, Calif. (CC of San Francisco)
68	Pendleton, Carl	DT	6'6"	277	RFr.	Sapulpa, Okla. (Sapulpa HS)
29	Peoples, Will	WR	6'1"	200	Sr.	Humble, Texas (Humble HS)
28	Perkins, Antonio	DB	6'0"	190	Sr.	Lawton, Okla. (Lawton HS)
28	Peterson, Adrian	RB	6'2"	210	Fr.	Palestine, Texas (Palestine HS)
51	Pleasant, Demarrio	LB	6'3"	222	RFr.	Lewisville, Texas (Lewisville HS)
23	Pool, Brodney	S	6'3"	208	Jr.	Houston, Texas (Westbury HS)
21	Poteat, Jowahn	DB	6'1"	197	Jr.	Ardmore, Okla. (Ardmore HS)
63	Quinn, J.D.	OL	6'2"	286	Fr.	Garland, Texas (Garland HS)
3	Rankins, Jejuan	WR	5'11"	180	Jr.	Windsor, N.C. (Bertie HS)
59	Rayl, Brett	OL	6'7"	304	Jr.	Lewisville, Texas (Lewisville HS)
75	Reid, Antonn	OL	6'3"	282	RFr.	Plano, Texas (Plano HS)
68	Rice, Jacob	DS	6'3"	225	Jr.	Norman, Okla. (Norman HS)
88	Roberts, Willie	TE	6'7"	245	Jr.	Miami, Fla. (Northeastern A&M CC)
5	Robinson, David	WR	5'7"	155	RFr.	DeSoto, Texas (Kimball HS)
65	Rothenberg, Aaron	OL	6'4"	290	So.	Madill, Okla. (Madill HS) 3
8	Runnels, J.D.	FB	6'1"	246	Jr.	Midwest City, Okla. (Carl Albert HS)
71	Schacht, Cameron	OL	6'5"	288	Fr.	Coppell, Texas (Coppell HS)
5	Shelby, Brandon	CB	5'11"	185	Sr.	Kansas City, Mo. (Rockhurst HS)
60	Sims, Wes	OL	6'5"	317	Sr.	Weatherford, Okla. (Weatherford HS)
25	Stephens, Darren	DB	6'3"	191	Sr.	Lewisville, Texas (Lewisville HS)
33	Strong, Fred	WR	6'3"	188	Fr.	Austin, Texas (Stephen F. Austin HS)
43	Stroud, Joseph	DB	5'9"	175	RFr.	Monroe, La.
99	Sublet, Vershun	DE	6'0"	255	Sr.	Lancaster, Texas (Lancaster HS)
30	Tennial, Courtney	RB	5'10"	228	RFr.	Glenpool, Okla. (Glen Pool HS)
58	Thibodeaux, Calvin	DE	6'1"	249	Jr.	Houston, Texas (Westbury HS)
12	Thompson, Paul	QB	6'4"	208	Jr.	Leander, Texas (Leander HS)
39	Townsend, Dan	FB	6'0"	234	So.	Sulphur, Okla. (Sulphur HS)
24	Walker, Marcus	DB	5'11"	180	Fr.	Waco, Texas (Waco HS)
18	White, Jason	QB	6'3"	226	Sr.	Tuttle, Okla. (Tuttle HS)
41	Williams, Darrien	S	6'0"	200	RFr.	Mesquite, Texas (North Mesquite HS)
98	Williams, John	DE	6'5"	242	RFr.	Houston, Texas (Lamar HS)
32	Wilson, Sadiki	WR	6'0"	215	Sr.	Oklahoma City, Okla. (Millwood HS)
4	Wilson, Travis	WR	6'3"	216	Jr.	Carrollton, Texas (Creekview HS)
25	Wolfe, D.J.	RB	5'11"	192	Fr.	Lawton, Okla. (Eisenhower HS)
40	Zaslaw, Dane	FB	6'2"	232	RFr.	Edmond, Okla. (Memorial HS)